The Whole Shebang Air Fryer Cookbook with Holiday Bonus

Brought to you by AirFrying.net

Introduction

For nearly five decades, healthcare authorities have been warning the public about the negative health effects of eating a diet high in saturated fats. More recently, nutritional experts have revealed the artery-clogging dangers of trans fat, with health risks ranging from diabetes to heart disease. With grave warnings like these, health-conscious individuals are faced with the difficult task of balancing hectic, stress-filled work days and family responsibilities with preparing healthy meals. With hot-button trends, like "meal prep", costly meal delivery services, and ever-conflicting dietary information, how does one sift through all the guidelines and manage to prepare healthy meals his or her family will love without spending hours in the kitchen?

Purchasing an air fryer is an optimal solution to these meal-prep woes.

An air fryer is a small appliance that, through rapid air technology, surrounds the food inside with hot air, cooking it to a crisp, fried texture while using only a fraction of the oil required by a deep fryer. Because an air fryer does not submerge the food in hot oil, air fried food absorbs only a minimal amount of the unhealthy fats. The result is delicious food with the same deep-fried texture you love but none of the unhealthy side effects.

In addition to health benefits, air frying is also faster and easier than cooking in the oven or deep fryer. The air fryer takes only 2-3 minutes to preheat to high temperatures, unlike an oven, which can take up to 15 minutes to preheat. The air fryer also cooks food more efficiently than an oven. The result is fast, delicious food you can prepare, cook and deliver to your table, often in less than 30 minutes.

Moreover, clean-up is fast and easy with an air fryer. Most brands are equipped with dishwasher safe parts and non-stick baskets that make clean up a breeze. Simply put the basket in the dishwasher or wipe with soapy water and rinse. When compared to scrubbing food residue from baking dishes, air fryer clean-up is a snap.

And the best part?

Air frying is not limited to a specific type of food. In fact, most any food can be cooked in an air fryer, depending upon its capacity size - from vegetables and meat to packaged frozen foods and even desserts! Add some variety to the hum-drum veggies in your meal rotation by air frying foods like asparagus, broccoli, potatoes and green beans and experimenting with different oils and spices. Impress the special people in your life with an elegant meal of air-fried scallops and filet mignon. Pressed for time? Preheat the air fryer and toss in some frozen French fries or tater tots for a quick side perfect with chicken tenders or burgers. With the proper attachments, even desserts like cake, brownies and turnovers can be cooked to perfection.

The sky is truly the limit with an air fryer, which AirFrying.net clearly demonstrates in our debut cookbook, featuring more than 100 recipes and our bonus holiday section. While some of the recipes featured in *The Whole Shebang Cookbook* can be found on our website, airfrying.net, the majority of these recipes have never been seen before. Plus, the holiday bonus will provide ideas for holiday meals that can be prepared conveniently in the air fryer to save you time and stress while entertaining, whether it's for Christmas or Thanksgiving feasts or gearing up for a Fourth of July cookout.

Thank you for purchasing our cookbook. For more information about air frying and for additional recipes, product reviews, tips and tricks, and videos, please visit our website, www.AirFrying.net.

Table of Contents

Introduction   2

Appetizers   9

Bang Bang Panko Shrimp	10	Mozzarella Cheese Sticks	18
Cream Cheese Wontons	11	Mussels in White Wine Sauce	19
Cheesy Chicken Quesadillas	12	Nachos Supreme	20
Crispy Chicken Wings	13	Potato Chips with Beer Cheese	21
Fried Green Tomatoes	14	Potato Skins, Fully Loaded	22
Blooming Onion	14	Spicy Southwest Egg Rolls	23
Fried Mushrooms	15	Spring Rolls	24
Fried Ravioli	15	Vegetarian Egg Rolls	25
Fried Pickles	16	Sausage Balls	26
Hush Puppies	17		

Breads   27

Cheddar Biscuits	28	Garlic Knots	32
Mini Banana Bread Loaves	29	Monkey Bread	33
Cheesy Garlic Pull Apart Bread	30	Fantastic Fry Bread	34
Best Biscuits Ever	31	Perfect Pretzel Bites	35
Corn Fritters	32	Pumpkin Bread	37

Breakfast   38

Breakfast Potatoes	39	Hard Boiled Eggs	46
Breakfast Quesadilla	40	Blueberry Bagels	47
Berry Good Morning Muffins	41	Low-Carb Crustless Quiche	47
Breakfast Egg Rolls	42	Rise & Shine Breakfast Pizza	48
Cinnamon Sugar Donuts	43	Sausage & Egg Sandwich	48
Eggs Benedict	44	Ultimate Cinnamon Toast	49
Sausage Patties	45	Van-Cin French Toast Sticks	50
Everybody Loves Bacon	45		

Dessert   51

Almond-Chocolate Biscotti	52	Cherry Hand Pies	59
Apple Dumplings	54	S'mores	59
Granny's Apple Fritters	55	Ultimate Chocolate Cake	60
Chocolate Chip Cookies	56	Sour Cream Banana Cake	61
Chocolate Soufflé	57	Caramel Frosting	61
Triple Berry Dessert Egg Rolls	58		

Main Dishes 62

Fish and Chips	63
Salmon w/ Lemon & Rosemary	64
Turkey Breast	65
Asian Ahi Tuna Steaks	66
Buttermilk Fried Chicken	67
Calabash Shrimp	68
Italian-Style Meatballs	69
Cajun Chicken Strips	70
Chicken Chimichangas	71
Classic Cheeseburgers	72
Crispy Chicken Parmesan	73
Coconut Shrimp	74
Cumin-Infused Chicken Thighs	75
Bacon-Wrapped Turkey Filets	76
Pork Chops with Apricot Glaze	77
Eggplant Parmesan	78
Fried Catfish	79
Honey Ginger Salmon	80
Sweet Whiskey-Glazed Ribs	81
Kickin' Kebabs	82
Lobster Tails for Two	82
Orange Chicken	83
Ragin' Cajun Shrimp	83
Roasted Whole Chicken	84
Sea Scallops	85
Stuffed Bell Peppers	86
Barbecue Drumsticks	87
Meatloaf	88

Sides 89

Multi-Colored Roasted Potatoes	90
Loaded "Baked" Potatoes	91
Bacon-Wrapped Asparagus	91
"Baked" Sweet Potatoes	92
Zesty Curly Fries	92
Beer-Battered Onion Rings	93
Brussels Sprouts with Marinade	94
Old-Fashioned French Fries	95
Green Beans with Garlic & Sage	96
Panko Parmesan Broccoli	97
Roasted Corn on the Cob	98
Sweet Potato Fries	99
Squash & Zucchini with Onions	100

Holiday Bonus Menus 101

Honey Glazed Spiral Ham	102
Turkey Breast	103
Apple-Bourbon Cornish Hens	104
Lamb Chops with Mint Jelly	105
Duck with Orange Sauce	106
Pork Tenderloin	107
Mummy Dogs	108
Whiskey Glazed Ribs	109
Classic Cheeseburgers	110
Hot Dogs	111
Healthy Turkey Burgers	112
Filets with Scallops	113
Orange-Cranberry Stuffing	114
Sweet Potato Casserole	115
Okra	116
Corn Pudding	116
Collard Greens	117
Honey-Glazed Carrots	118
Baked Beans	119
Garlic Parmesan Corn	119
Potato Latkes	120
Holiday Sugar Cookies	121
Honey Cake	122
Cranberry Swirl Cheesecake	123
Baked Apples or Pears	124
Chocolate Soufflé	125
Red Velvet Cake	126
Pumpkin Soufflé	127
Cream Puffs	128
Patriot Fruit Pizza	129

Appetizers

Bang Bang Panko Shrimp

Ingredients for Shrimp:
- ½-1 pound of raw shrimp, peeled and deveined
- 1 egg, beaten
- ¼ – ½ cup all-purpose flour
- 1 cup panko bread crumbs
- 1-1½ tsp. paprika
- Salt and pepper to taste
- Coconut oil spray

Ingredients for Bang Bang Sauce:
- ½ cup plain Greek yogurt or coconut yogurt
- 1 Tbsp. sriracha sauce
- ¼ cup sweet chili sauce

Directions:
- Sprinkle the shrimp with the salt, pepper, and paprika.
- Dip the shrimp in the flour, followed by the egg wash, and then the panko bread crumbs.
- Place shrimp in the air fryer. Cook at 400 degrees for 8 minutes, flipping halfway through.
- While the shrimp is cooking, mix together the yogurt, sriracha sauce and the sweet chili sauce in a medium bowl. Serve with the shrimp as a condiment or pour over the shrimp as a sauce.

Cream Cheese Wontons

Ingredients:
- 1 package wonton wrappers
- 8 oz. cream cheese, softened
- ½ tsp. of sugar or favorite sweetener
- ½ tsp. onion powder
- 1 egg, beaten

Directions:
- In a medium-sized bowl, stir together cream cheese, sugar, and onion powder until smooth.
- Spoon cheese mixture into center of the eggroll wrapper, folding ends together and seal with the egg wash, repeating until mixture is gone.
- Spritz air fryer basket with oil and place wontons inside.
- Cook at 400 degrees for 8 minutes.

Eat plain or serve with sweet & sour sauce.

Cheesy Chicken Quesadillas

Ingredients:
- 1 package pre-cooked grilled chicken
- 1 yellow pepper
- 1 orange pepper
- 8 oz. bag of shredded cheese
- 1 yellow onion
- Medium size tortilla soft shells
- Olive oil spray

Directions:
- Slice yellow and orange peppers and dice onion.
- Spray olive oil on bottom of air fryer cooking pot.
- Place 1 tortilla shell in air fryer pot.
- Spread cheese, chicken, onions, and peppers over tortilla shell.
- Put another tortilla shell on top of ingredients.
- Put in air fryer at 370 degrees for 3 minutes.
- Flip tortilla shell and put back in air fryer at 370 degrees for 3 minutes.
- Remove from air fryer, slice and enjoy!

Serve with guacamole, salsa and a dollop of sour cream.

Crispy Chicken Wings with Creole Spices

Ingredients:
- 3 pound bag frozen chicken wings
- 1 Tbsp. of your favorite creole seasoning blend
- Cooking spray

Instructions:
- Preheat air fryer to 400 degrees.
- Spray basket with non-stick cooking spray or mist with favorite oil.
- Place frozen wings in a single layer in the basket and cook at 400 for five minutes.
- Remove basket and sprinkle with creole seasoning.
- Return to heat and air fry for an additional 20 minutes, turning the wings once.

Serve with celery and ranch or your favorite dipping sauce.

Fried Green Tomatoes

Ingredients:
- 3-4 green tomatoes
- 1 cup all-purpose flour
- ½ cup corn meal
- ½ cup bread crumbs
- 2 tsp. salt
- ¼ tsp. pepper
- ¼ tsp. paprika
- 2 eggs
- ½ cup buttermilk

Directions:
- Using a kitchen knife or mandoline slicer, slice tomatoes into ¼ inch slices.
- In a small bowl, beat together eggs, buttermilk, salt, pepper, and paprika.
- In another bowl, mix together cornmeal and bread crumbs.
- Dust tomato slices in flour, dunk in the egg/milk mixture, and then dust in the cornmeal/bread crumb mixture.
- Place coated tomatoes in a single layer in the air fryer basket. Repeat until all tomato slices are coated.
- Cook at 400 degrees for 8 minutes, flipping once.

Blooming Onion

Ingredients:
- 1 large Vidalia onion
- 1 ¼ cup all-purpose flour
- 1 tsp. baking powder
- 2 tsp. kosher salt
- Pepper and paprika, to taste
- 1 ¼ cups of your favorite beer

Instructions:
- Cut the onion 8 times across and 8 times lengthwise without cutting all the way through the end of it. Separate the layers until the onion looks like a blossom.
- In a large bowl, mix together flour, baking powder, salt, pepper, and paprika.
- Gradually add beer, mixing until a batter-like consistency is achieved.
- Place the onion in the batter, using a spoon to cover all areas of the onion.
- Cook at 400 degrees for 30 minutes.

Serve with horseradish sauce or spicy ranch.

Fried Mushrooms with Parmesan & Italian Spices

Ingredients:
- 2 cartons of fresh, whole mushrooms
- 1 cup flour
- ¼ tsp. salt and 1/8 tsp pepper
- ½ tsp. Italian seasoning
- A pinch of garlic powder
- ¼ cup parmesan cheese
- 1 egg, beaten
- 1 cup buttermilk

Directions:
- In a medium-sized bowl, combine flour, cheese, and spices. Set aside.
- In a small bowl, mix together the egg and buttermilk.
- Dip mushrooms, one at a time, in the egg wash and then coat in the flour mixture.
- Spray basket with non-stick cooking spray or mist with your favorite oil.
- Place mushrooms in a single layer in the air fryer basket.
- Cook at 400 for 5 minutes, turning once.

Serve with horseradish dipping sauce or marinara.

Fried Ravioli

Ingredients:
- 1 bag cheese ravioli.
- ½ cup grated parmesan cheese
- ½ Italian seasoning
- 1 egg, beaten

Directions:
- Mix together parmesan cheese and Italian seasoning.
- Dip ravioli, one at a time, in the beaten egg and then coat with the parmesan cheese mixture.
- Spray air fryer basket with non-stick cooking spray or sprits with your favorite oil.
- Cook at 400 degrees for 10 minutes, turning once.

Serve with marinara sauce for dipping.

Fried Pickles with Cajun Seasoning

Ingredients:
- 1 jar of your favorite dill pickle chips
- 2 eggs, beaten
- 1 cup almond flour
- 1 tsp. Cajun seasoning (or to taste)
- 1/2 tsp. salt
- 1/4 tsp. black pepper

Directions:
- In a small bowl, beat two eggs. Set aside.
- On a large plate, mix together almond flour and seasonings.
- Spray the basket of your air fryer with cooking spray (or mist with your favorite oil—avocado is our recommendation)
- Dip the dill pickles in the egg wash, no more than two or three at a time.
- Immediately coat with flour mixture.
- Place in air fryer basket.
- Mist with cooking spray or your favorite oil.
- Cook at 400 degrees for 8-10 minutes, turning once.

If you're not counting carbs, you can replace the almond flour with panko crumbs.

Serve with spicy ranch dressing or horseradish sauce

Hush Puppies

Ingredients:
- 1 cup corn meal (yellow)
- 2/3 cup all-purpose flour
- 2 tsp. sugar
- 1 tsp. salt
- 2 tsp. baking powder
- 2 eggs, beaten in a separate bowl
- ¾ cup milk
- 2 Tbsp. vegetable oil
- ½ small onion, minced
- Optional: red and green pepper, to taste (minced)

Directions:
- In a large bowl, mix together corn meal, flour, sugar, baking powder, and salt.
- In a separate bowl, beat together eggs, adding milk and vegetable oil until well-blended.
- Mix egg mixture with the dry ingredients and add the onion and green peppers.
- Roll 2 Tbsp of dough mixture into small balls and place into air fryer basket in a single layer.
- Air fry at 400 degrees for 8 minutes, turning once, or until golden brown.

Serve with honey butter for dipping.

Mozzarella Cheese Sticks

Ingredients:
- 4 mozzarella cheese sticks
- 1 cup of panko crumbs
- 2 eggs
- 1 tsp. garlic powder
- 1/4 tsp. salt
- 1/2 tsp. Italian seasoning

Directions:
- Cut cheese sticks on half.
- In a small bowl, beat together eggs, salt, garlic powder and Italian seasoning.
- Pour panko crumbs on a plate.
- Dip cheese sticks in egg mixture then roll in panko crumbs, making sure the cheese stick is well-coated.
- Place coated cheese sticks in the freezer for 20-30 minutes.
- Spray air fryer basket with non-stick cooking spray.
- Place cheese sticks in air fryer. Coat tops with cooking spray.
- Cook at 400 degrees for 5 minutes.

Serve with marinara sauce for dipping.

Mussels in White Wine Sauce

Ingredients:
- 2-3 lbs. fresh mussels
- 1 Tbsp. olive oil
- 1 small red onion
- 3 cloves garlic, minced
- 2 Tbsp. chopped fresh parsley
- 1 cup dry white wine
- ¼ tsp. sea salt
- 1 Tbsp. fresh lemon juice

Directions:
- Wash the mussels in cold water, discarding those with open or broken shells.
- In an air fryer-safe attachment, mix together olive oil, onion, garlic, parsley, white wine, salt, and lemon juice; add about half the mussels, depending upon the size of your air fryer.
- Cook at 400 degrees for 3-5 minutes, or until shells have opened.

Nachos Supreme

Ingredients:
- 1 bag of 6-inch corn tortillas
- 1 Tbsp avocado oil
- Sea salt or Seasoned salt to taste
- Optional: cooking spray

Directions:
- Cut the tortillas into triangles.
- Brush oil onto each triangle and sprinkle lightly with salt.
- Transfer tortilla triangles to your air fryer basket. (You can spray the basket with cooking spray if you'd like.)
- Cook at 350 degrees for 8 minutes, shaking the basket halfway through.
- Top with refried beans, queso sauce, tomatoes, guacamole and sour cream.

Potato Chips with Beer Cheese

Ingredients:
- 4-5 baking-style potatoes
- 1 Tbsp. vegetable oil (I use olive)
- Salt and pepper to taste
- Optional: your favorite seasonings, like ranch or cheddar.
- Cooking spray (if needed)

Directions:
- Peel potatoes and slice into thin coins. Use a vegetable slicer for faster results.
- Place sliced potato rounds in a large bowl.
- Toss with oil.
- Add salt, pepper, and seasonings, and toss together.
- If needed for your air fryer brand, mist the basket with cooking spray.
- Transfer potatoes to your air fryer basket.
- Cook at 390 degrees for 20 minutes, shaking every 5-7 minutes. If the potatoes are not as crispy as you'd like, cook for an additional 5 minutes.

Ingredients for Beer Cheese:
- ½ tsp. garlic powder
- 1/8 tsp. cayenne pepper
- 1 tsp. Dijon mustard (add more to taste)
- 3 Tbsp. flour

- Salt to taste
- 2 Tbsp. butter
- 3 cups cheddar cheese
- ¾ cup whole milk or half and half
- ½ cup beer (we recommend a good Pilsner)

Directions for Beer Cheese:
- In a medium saucepan, melt the butter over medium heat and gradually add the flour, whisking together.
- Remove pan from heat and gradually add the milk or half and half, whisking together until smooth.
- Stir in spices, mustard, and beer. Return pan to heat, cooking over medium heat. Stir frequently until the mixture is smooth, thick, and bubbling.
- Add the cheese, one cup at a time, stirring until melted.
- Pour into a serving bowl and serve with lightly salted chips

Potato Skins, Fully Loaded

Ingredients:
- 5 baking potatoes
- 1 cup cheddar cheese
- 5-8 strips bacon, cooked and crumbled
- ¼ cup chives, chopped
- Salt and pepper to taste
- Sour cream to taste
- Ranch dressing to taste

Directions:
- Air fry or bake whole potatoes according to air fryer manual or, if baked, at 425 degrees for approximately one hour.
- When cooked thoroughly, cut open potatoes lengthwise and scoop out the inside. (Save the insides for mashed potatoes or potato cakes!)
- Sprinkle cheese, bacon and chives on the potato skins.
- Place in your air fryer basket in a single layer and cook at 375 for 5-7 minutes, or until the cheese is melted.

Drizzle with ranch dressing and top with sour cream and extra chives, if desired.

Spicy Southwest Egg Rolls

Ingredients:
- 1 cup cooked chicken (for quicker prep, you can use canned or leave out chicken for vegetarian option)
- 1 cup canned black beans, drained.
- 1 cup canned corn, drained.
- ¼ cup spinach, frozen
- 2 cups taco blend or jalapeno cheddar cheese, shredded
- 1 Tbsp. garlic powder
- ½ tsp onion powder
- ½ tsp chili powder
- ½ tsp cumin, ground
- Salt to taste
- 1 package egg roll wrappers

Directions:
- In a large skillet or wok, cook chicken, beans, corn and spinach until heated through.
- Drain.
- Return to skillet and add spices until thoroughly blended.
- Stir in cheese and then transfer mixture to a large bowl.
- Scoop approximately ¼ cup of mixture onto the center of the egg roll wrappers and seal them.
- Spritz basket with oil and place egg rolls in a single layer. Spritz top of egg rolls with oil.
- Cook at 390 degrees for 8 minutes, turning halfway.

Serve with southwest ranch or chipotle dressing.

Spring Rolls

Ingredients:
- 1 bag coleslaw mix (the kind with carrots included)
- 1 tsp. fresh ginger
- 1 green onion
- 1 Tbsp. soy sauce
- 1 Tbsp. rice wine
- Salt and pepper to taste
- 1 package spring roll wrappers

Directions:
- In a large skillet or wok, cook cabbage and green onion, adding soy sauce, rice wine, salt, and pepper.
- Transfer ingredients to a large bowl.
- Scoop one Tbsp. of mixture and place in spring roll wrappers, sealing according to the package directions.
- Then, spritz the basket of your air fryer with oil and place spring rolls in a single layer. Spritz the tops of the wrappers with oil.
- Cook at 390 degrees for 5-8 minutes, turning once.

Serve with shrimp sauce or sweet & sour sauce.

Vegetarian Egg Rolls

Ingredients:
- 3 cups shredded cabbage
- 1 large shredded carrot (you can use one package of coleslaw mix to save prep time, replacing the cabbage and carrot)
- 3-4 whole mushrooms, diced
- 3 cloves garlic, chopped
- 1 Tbsp. vegetable or sesame oil
- 1 tsp. sesame oil
- 1 Tbsp. soy sauce
- 1/4 tsp. sugar
- Salt to taste
- Egg roll wrappers (located in the produce department at most grocery stores)
- 1 Tbsp. cornstarch
- 1/4 cup cold water

Directions:
- In a small bowl, whisk together the cold water and cornstarch. Set aside.
- In a large non-stick skillet or wok, heat the vegetable oil and add cabbage, carrots, mushrooms and garlic. Sauté until tender.
- Add the sesame oil, soy sauce, sugar and salt. Sauté another 2-3 minutes until the filling is well mixed. Drain and place mixture into a large bowl.
- On a flat surface, turn the egg roll wrapper in a diamond shape, spooning 3 tablespoons of the filling into the center of the wrapper. Fold tightly until your wrapper looks like an open envelop.
- Seal edges with cornstarch mixture. Continue rolling tightly and seal again with the cornstarch mixture.

- Repeat until filling is gone.
- Spray the basket of your air fryer with cooking spray. In a single layer, place egg rolls in basket. Spray the tops of the egg rolls with cooking spray.
- Cook at 390 degrees for 8 minutes.

Serve with sweet & sour sauce.

Sausage Balls

Ingredients:
- ½ pound breakfast sausage (we use mild, but buy spicy if you prefer it)
- 1 cup Bisquick or bread crumbs (you can use Italian crumbs for added flavor)
- 2 cups extra sharp cheddar cheese

Directions:
- Mix together sausage and Bisquick. Then, add the cheese, mixing thoroughly.
- Roll about 2 Tbsp. of mixture into a ball; repeat with all of the mixture.
- Spritz air fryer basket with your favorite oil and add the sausage balls in a single layer. Then spritz their tops with oil.
- Cook at 375 for 12-15 minutes, shaking once.

For a low carb option, replace the Bisquick with crushed pork rinds.

Breads

Cheddar Biscuits

Ingredients:
- 2 cups all-purpose flour
- 2 tsp. sugar
- 1 Tbsp. baking powder
- 2 tsp. garlic powder
- ½ tsp. salt
- 1 cup buttermilk
- 1 ½ cups shredded cheddar
- 2 Tbsp. butter, melted
- 2 additional Tbsp. butter, melted, for topping
- ¼ cup chopped parsley for topping

Directions:
- In a large mixing bowl, combine dry ingredients.
- Add buttermilk, mixing thoroughly.
- Add cheddar and melted butter, stirring until well-combined.
- In an air-fryer safe baking dish, drop approximately 2 spoonfuls of biscuit mixture for each biscuit onto the pan or dish.
- Cook at 400 degrees for 8-10 minutes.
- Brush with butter and sprinkle with parsley.

Mini Banana Bread Loaves

Ingredients:
- 1 ½ cups ripe bananas, mashed
- 5 eggs
- 2 cups flour
- 2 tsp. baking soda
- 2 cups sugar
- 2 tsp. cinnamon
- 1 cup walnuts (optional)
- 6 Tbsp. buttermilk
- 1 cup butter, softened

Directions:
- Using a stand or hand mixer, mix together softened butter and sugar; add eggs one at a time.
- Slowly add flour, baking soda, cinnamon and buttermilk.
- Stir in bananas and walnuts.

- Pour into four mini loaf pans, filling ¾ way to top.
- Cook loaves 1-2 at a time in the air fryer at 350 degrees for 25-28 minutes.
- Cool on wire racks for 10 minutes.

These make great holiday gifts for friends, neighbors and teachers when you place in decorative tins or bags and attach a bow.

Cheesy Garlic Pull-Apart Bread

Ingredients:
- 16 dinner rolls, frozen
- 1 ½ tsp. garlic powder
- ½ tsp. onion powder
- 1 tsp. parsley flakes
- ½ tsp. Italian seasoning
- ½ tsp. salt
- ½ cup butter, melted
- ½ cup grated parmesan cheese
- ½ cup grated romano cheese

Directions:
- Thaw rolls for around 30 minutes until you can pull them apart. Using a clean pair of kitchen shears, cut rolls in half.
- Mix the dry seasoning ingredients together.
- Place roll halves in air fryer-safe pan and pour the melted butter and seasoning ingredients over the rolls, topping with the parmesan and romano cheeses. Leave dough out at room temperature until it rises.
- Place pan in air fryer and cook at 360 for approximately 15-20 minutes. Check progress at around 10 minutes to prevent overcooking.

Best Biscuits Ever

Ingredients:
- 2 cups all-purpose flour
- ¼ tsp. baking soda
- 1 Tbsp. baking powder
- 1 tsp. salt
- 6 Tbsp. unsalted butter, cut into cubes
- 1 cup buttermilk

Directions:
- In the bowl of your food processor, combine all dry ingredients.
- Add butter cubes and pulse until coarse.
- Add buttermilk.
- On a floured cloth or board, work the dough, gently patting until it reaches the desired thickness. Then, using a biscuit cutter, cut the biscuits.
- In an air fryer-safe pan, "bake" the biscuits at 400 for 8-10 minutes.

Great for sausage biscuits, biscuits and gravy, or served with jelly or apple butter.

Corn Fritters

Ingredients:
- 1 can creamed corn
- 2 eggs, beaten
- 2 ½ cups all-purpose flour
- 2 tsp. baking powder
- 1 tsp. salt
- ¾ cup milk
- 2 Tbsp. melted butter

Directions:
- In a large bowl, mix together all ingredients.
- Spritz air fryer basket with your favorite oil.
- Using a tablespoon for measurement, place lumps of the mixture in a single layer in the air fryer basket.
- Cook at 390-400 degrees for 6 minutes, turning halfway through.

Garlic Knots with Olive Oil & Parsley

Ingredients:
- 4 cloves garlic, minced
- 1 tsp. salt
- 3 Tbsp. olive oil
- 1 14 oz. refrigerated pizza crust (or make your own if you prefer)
- 2 Tbsp. parmesan or parmesan-romano cheese, grated
- 1 tsp. Italian seasoning

Directions:
- In a medium sized bowl, mix together garlic, Italian seasoning, parsley and olive oil. Set aside.
- Roll out pizza dough onto a cutting board or flat surface and slice dough into thin strips. Then, roll the dough into "knots".
- Dip the dough in the oil and garlic mixture and place, 6-8 at a time (depending upon your air fryer capacity), in an oiled air fryer basket. Sprinkle with salt.
- Cook at 400 for 3-4 minutes or until golden brown.
- Dust with parmesan.

Serve with marinara sauce for dipping.

Monkey Bread

Ingredients:
- 1 can refrigerated biscuits
- ¼ cup sugar
- 3 Tbsp. brown sugar
- 1 tsp. cinnamon
- ¼ tsp. nutmeg
- 4 Tbsp. butter, melted

Directions:
- In a small bowl, mix white and brown sugar, cinnamon, and nutmeg. Set aside.
- Cut each biscuit into fourths.
- Dip each piece of biscuit into the butter and roll in the sugar/spice mixture until well coated.
- Place each coated piece in a round or square baking pan that fits inside your air fryer, stacking until gone.
- Cook at 400 degrees for 5-8 minutes, or until golden brown.

Perfect served with coffee at breakfast or for dessert.

Fantastic Fry Bread

Ingredients:
- 2 cups all-purpose flour
- 1 Tbsp. baking powder
- 1 tsp. salt
- 1 cup milk
- Optional: additional herbs and spices for added flavor

Directions:
- Preheat your air fryer to 365 degrees.
- In a large bowl, stir together all ingredients (adding milk gradually) or mix in a stand mixer, using a dough hook.
- Remove the dough and knead on a floured surface. Let rest for five minutes.
- Divide dough into four rounds.
- Spritz air fryer basket with oil.
- Place rounds, one at a time, in the air fryer. Cook for six minutes (or until golden brown), flipping halfway through.

This delicious fry bread is diverse and can be served with a variety of foods. Top with beans, taco meat and cheese for Mexican cuisine, use as a delicious crust for pizza or Italian cheese bread, or serve with tzatziki sauce for a Mediterranean snack.

Perfect Pretzel Bites

Ingredients:
- 1 1/2 cups warm water
- 2 tablespoons light brown sugar
- 1 package active dry yeast (2 1/4 teaspoons)
- 3 ounces unsalted butter, melted
- 2 1/2 tsp. kosher salt
- 4 1/2 to 5 cups all-purpose flour
- Vegetable oil
- 3 quarts water
- 1/3 cup baking soda (for boiling the pretzels)
- 1 whole egg, beaten with 1 tablespoon cold water
- Coarse sea salt
- Optional: replace course sea salt topping with cinnamon and sugar for a sweet, rather than salty, treat.

Directions:
- Combine the water, sugar, yeast, and butter in the bowl of a stand mixer and mix, using a dough hook. Let sit for 5 minutes.
- Add the salt and flour and mix on low speed until combined. Increase the speed to medium and continue kneading until smooth.
- Remove the dough; place on a flat surface and knead into a ball.

- In a large bowl, pour in oil. Then, adding the dough, turn dough over and over until well-coated. Cover the dough and allow it to rise for about an hour.
- Preheat the air fryer to 400 degrees.
- Bring the 3 quarts of water to a boil in a small roasting pan over high heat and carefully add the baking soda. Watch closely to avoid boiling over.
- Remove the dough from the bowl and place on a flat surface. Divide the dough into 8 equal pieces. Roll each piece into a long rope. Cut the dough into one-inch pieces to make the pretzel bites.
- Boil the pretzel bites in the baking soda solution a dozen or so at a time for around 30 seconds. Remove with a large slotted spoon.
- Then, spritz your air fryer with oil and place the pretzel bites in a single layer and brush the tops with egg wash. Sprinkle with salt.
- Cook for 10-12 minutes or until golden brown.
- Let cool for 10 minutes.

For a sweeter treat, you can dust with cinnamon and sugar instead of the salt before air frying.

Serve with mustard, cheese, or, if you seasoned with cinnamon and sugar, icing for dipping.

Pumpkin Bread

Ingredients:
- 1 box pumpkin bread mix
- 1 can pumpkin puree
- 4 large eggs
- 1 cup water
- ½ cup vegetable oil
- Optional: Chocolate chips, raisins, or nuts

Directions:
- Preheat air fryer to 365 degrees.
- Prepare pumpkin batter according to directions on box.
- Pour into mini loaf pans compatible with your air fryer.
- Cook two loaves at a time for 20-25 minutes.

Perfect for a delicious fall breakfast and oh, so delicious with coffee.

Breakfast

Breakfast Potatoes

Ingredients:
- 2-3 potatoes or ½ bag frozen diced potatoes
- 1 onion, diced
- 1 red pepper, diced
- 1 tsp. garlic powder
- ½ tsp. onion powder
- ½ tsp. paprika
- 1 tsp. salt
- 1 Tbsp. or spritz of your favorite oil

Directions:
- In a large bowl, mix together all ingredients.
- Toss or spritz the vegetables with a light coating of oil.
- Place vegetables in basket of your air fryer.
- Cook at 390 degrees for 15-20 minutes, shaking often.

Breakfast Quesadilla

Ingredients:
- 4 eggs, beaten and scrambled
- 1 cup diced ham
- 1 cup taco blend shredded cheese
- ½ onion, diced
- 1 green pepper, diced

Directions:
- Preheat your air fryer to 370 degrees.
- Spritz basket with avocado oil.
- Place one tortilla in bottom of basket. Then, layer with cheese, egg, ham, onion, pepper then top with more cheese.
- Top with second tortilla and mist with avocado oil.
- Cook at 370 for 6 minutes, flipping halfway through.

You can also use bacon or sausage or add more vegetables.
Serve with salsa, fresh avocado and sour cream.

Berry Good Morning Muffins

Ingredients:
- 1 ½ cups cake flour
- ½ cup sugar
- 1/3 cup vegetable oil
- 2 eggs
- 2 tsp. vanilla extract
- 1 cup blueberries, strawberries (diced), raspberries or blackberries, washed thoroughly. (Another option is to add one cup of mixed berries of your choice)

Directions:
- Preheat air fryer to 360 degrees.
- In a large mixing bowl, stir or whisk together oil, eggs, and vanilla extract.
- Add dry ingredients and stir until well-combined.
- Fold in berries.
- Line air fryer basket with muffin liners.
- Fill liners until ¾ full.
- Optional: sprinkle with cinnamon and brown sugar
- "Bake" in air fryer for 10-12 minutes.
- Plate and enjoy!

Breakfast Egg Rolls

Ingredients:
- 6 eggs, beaten and scrambled
- ¼ pound breakfast sausage crumbles
- ½ cup shredded cheese
- 8 egg roll wrappers
- ¼ tsp. cornstarch
- ½ cup cold water

Directions:
- Preheat your air fryer to 400.
- To make the egg mixture, cook breakfast sausage. Then add eggs, scrambling together.
- Allow mixture to cool until warm, rather than piping hot.
- Meanwhile, mix together cornstarch and cold water in a small bowl.
- Once cooled, add 2-3 spoonsful of the mixture to egg roll wrapper. Top with cheese.
- Fold eggroll wrapper, using the cornstarch mixture to seal.
- Mist eggroll with sesame oil.
- Repeat. This recipe should make approximately 8 egg rolls.
- Cook at 400 degrees for 8 minutes, turning once.

Add veggies like diced onion and bell pepper to your beaten eggs before scrambling. Serve with salsa, avocado, and a dollop of Greek yogurt or sour cream.

Cinnamon Sugar Donuts

Ingredients:
- 1 can of flaky layers biscuits
- 3-4 Tbsp. melted butter
- 1/4 cup granulated sugar
- 3 Tbsp. of brown sugar
- 1 tsp. of cinnamon (or to taste)
- 1/4 tsp. pumpkin pie spice

Directions:
- Open the can of biscuits and cut a small hole from the middle, using a knife, bottle cap, or 1-inch biscuit cutter.
- In a small bowl, mix together sugars and spices.
- Coat the basket of your air fryer with a few mists of oil or non-stick spray.
- Place the donuts in the air fryer, four at a time, depending on the size of your air fryer.
- Cook the donuts at 350 degrees for 5 minutes, turning twice for even cooking.
- Meanwhile, melt the three tablespoons of butter.
- You may want to pour the sugar mixture on a plate for easier coverage.
- Remove the donuts from the air fryer, brushing them with butter.
- Dip in the sugar mixture.

You can also cook the donut holes at 350 degrees for 3 minutes.

Eggs Benedict

Ingredients:
- 2 eggs
- 2 slices Canadian bacon
- 1 English muffin, cut in half
- ¼ cup salted butter, melted
- 3 egg yolks
- 1 Tbsp. lemon juice
- Salt and pepper to taste
- Pinch of cayenne pepper

Directions:
- Spray an air fryer-safe ramekin and crack an egg into it.
- Place ramekin, as well as 1 slice Canadian bacon, in air fryer and cook at 325 degrees for 3 minutes; remove and set aside.
- Toast the English muffin in the air fryer, cooking at 370 for around 2-3 minutes, or until it reaches the desired crispness.
- Repeat for another serving.
- In a blender, mix together melted butter, egg yolks, lemon juice, salt, pepper and cayenne pepper until smooth.
- Pour into a microwave safe bowl.
- Microwave for 15-20 seconds.

Plating Instructions:
- On a small plate, place the toasted English muffin half, flat side up.
- Top with the Canadian bacon then add the baked egg layer.
- Drizzle with hollandaise sauce.

Sausage Patties

Ingredients:
- ½ pound of your favorite brand and flavor sausage patties (we like maple)

Directions:
- Mist your air fryer basket with your favorite oil.
- If you have a tube of sausage, cut into ¼ inch rounds and place in air fryer basket. Otherwise, shape into patties.
- Cook at 400 degrees for 8-10 minutes, flipping halfway.

Everybody Loves Bacon

Ingredients:
- 4 slices of your favorite brand and flavor of bacon

Directions:
- Cook bacon at 350 for 8-10 minutes.

You can increase heat and reduce cooking time for crispier texture.

Hard Boiled Eggs

Ingredients:
- 6 eggs

Directions:
- Place the wire rack that came with your air fryer or air fryer accessory kit in the basket of your air fryer.
- Place all six eggs on the wire rack.
- Cook at 250 for 18-20 minutes.
- Remove eggs and put them in an ice water bath.
- Peel and enjoy!

Blueberry Bagels

Ingredients:
- 1 cup cake flour (self-rising)
- 1 cup blueberry Greek yogurt
- 1 egg, beaten

Directions:
- In a large mixing bowl, mix together flour and blueberry yogurt.
- Sprinkle a flat surface with flour and roll dough into a ball.
- Cut dough into fourths.
- Roll by hand to form a bagel ring, pinching ends together.
- Mist air fryer basket with oil.
- Place bagel rings, 2 at a time, in the basket; brush with egg.
- Cook at 330 for 9-10 minutes.
- Let cool.

Top with cream cheese, butter or jelly.

Low-Carb Crustless Quiche

Ingredients:
- 6 eggs, beaten
- 3 oz colby jack shredded cheese
- 1 cup diced ham
- 2 cups fresh spinach, sautéed until tender
- Salt and pepper to taste

Directions
- In a large mixing bowl, stir together all ingredients.
- Spritz an air fryer-safe pie plate with your favorite oil.
- Pour egg mixture into pie plate.
- Cook at 350 for 20-25 minutes.

Rise & Shine Breakfast Pizza

Ingredients
- Small personal sized pizza crust (or one pita bread)
- 2-3 Tbsp. pizza sauce or salsa
- 2-3 eggs, beaten and scrambled
- ¼ cup cooked sausage or bacon crumbles
- ½ cup mozzarella cheese, shredded

Directions:
- Place pizza crust on an air fryer-safe pizza pan.
- Top crust with sauce.
- Layer with egg, sausage and/or bacon, and cheese.
- Cook at 400 for 5-10 minutes, or until cheese is melted and crust is golden brown.

Sausage & Egg Breakfast Sandwich

Ingredients:
- 2 eggs, cooked to your preference (scrambled, sunny side up, etc.)
- 2 sausage patties, cooked (Bacon, ham, or Canadian bacon also works)
- 2 slices sourdough bread (or your favorite bread)
- 1 Tbsp. butter
- Optional: 2 slices of your favorite cheese

Directions:
- Mist your air fryer basket with oil of your choice.
- Preheat air fryer to 400 degrees while prepping eggs and sausage.
- Butter both sides of sourdough bread.
- Place first sourdough slice in air fryer basket.
- Layer with eggs, sausage patties and cheese.
- Top with second sourdough slice.
- Cook at 400 for 4 minutes, flipping halfway. (You may want to increase or decrease time, based on desired texture).

We like to add a couple slices of fresh tomato during the summer months.

Ultimate Cinnamon Toast

Ingredients:
- 1-2 slices of your favorite bread
- 1 tsp. cinnamon
- 1 tsp. brown sugar
- 1 tsp. granulated sugar
- 1 Tbsp. butter

Directions:
- In a small bowl, mix together cinnamon, brown sugar, and regular sugar. Set aside.
- Butter both sides of bread slices.
- Place bread inside air fryer basket and sprinkle with cinnamon-sugar mixture.
- Cook at 400 for approximately 3 minutes or until desired texture is achieved.

Vanilla-Cinnamon French Toast Sticks

Ingredients:
- 2-4 slices thick-sliced Italian-style bread
- 2 eggs, beaten
- ¼ tsp. vanilla extract
- 1 tsp. cinnamon
- ½ tsp. sugar

Directions:
- Cut bread into 1-inch vertical strips.
- Mix together beaten eggs, vanilla, cinnamon and sugar.
- Dip bread strips into egg mixture then place in oiled air fryer basket.
- Air fry at 360 degrees for approximately 6 minutes, flipping halfway.

Serve with maple syrup or vanilla icing.

Desserts

Almond-Chocolate Biscotti

Ingredients:
- 1 ¼ cups coarsely chopped, toasted almonds
- 2 cups all-purpose flour
- 1 Tbsp. all-purpose flour
- 1 cup light brown sugar, tightly packed
- 1 tsp. baking powder
- ½ tsp. cinnamon
- ½ tsp. salt
- 1 tsp. almond extract
- ¼ cup butter, cubed
- 3 eggs
- 1 Tbsp. melted coconut oil
- ¼ cup dark chocolate chunks
- Egg wash: 1 beaten egg with 1 Tbsp. whole milk

Directions:
- In a large mixing bowl, whisk together flour, butter cubes, sugar, baking soda, cinnamon, and salt.
- Use a pastry cutter to achieve a crumbly mixture.
- Add almonds and dark chocolate chunks.
- In another bowl, whisk eggs, oil, and almond extract together; add to dry ingredients, stirring until just moistened.
- Flour your countertop or other flat surface and turn the dough, kneading until soft. With floured hands, cut dough into two halves.
- On a greased air fryer safe baking pan, place one of the halves, shaping into a loaf, flattening until around ½ inch thick.
- Brush with egg wash on tops and sides.
- "Bake" at 325 for 20 minutes or until sides and top are golden brown.
- Remove from air fryer and cool for 10-12 minutes on a wire rack.
- Once cooled, cut cookie loaf into long strips.
- Return to air fryer and cook for an additional 7-8 minutes. Turn and cook or an additional 3-5 minutes, or until desired texture is achieved.
- Remove from heat and let cool on wire racks.
- Plate and serve with coffee for dunking!

Apple Dumplings

Ingredients:
- 2 apples, peeled and cored
- 1 Tbsp. brown sugar
- 2 sheets puff pastry (found in frozen section of grocery store)
- 2 Tbsp. butter
- optional: cinnamon to taste

Directions:
- Lay puff pastry out flat.
- Put cored apple in center of puff pastry.
- Place brown sugar, butter and cinnamon into center of cored apples.
- Fold pastry over and roll up the sides into a circular shape around the apples.
- Brush melted butter onto pastry.
- Cook in air fryer at 365 degrees for 12 minutes.
- Flip dumpling over.
- Continue cooking for 12-13 additional minutes.
- Plate and enjoy with ice cream or whipped cream!

Granny's Apple Fritters

Ingredients:
- 1 cup apples, diced
- 1 egg
- 1 ¾ cups flour
- 2 tsp. baking powder
- ¼ cup of oil
- 1 cup milk
- Powdered sugar for dusting

Directions:
- Preheat air fryer to 390 degrees.
- In a large bowl, mix together flour and baking powder. Stir in diced apples.
- In a small bowl or measuring cup, add milk then stir in egg.
- Add wet mixture to dry mixture and combine until just moistened.
- Mist the air fryer basket with vegetable oil and drop spoonsful of batter into the basket. Mist tops of fritters with vegetable oil.
- Cook at 390 for 2-4 minutes, turning once.
- Top with powdered sugar.

Serve with cinnamon apple butter for dipping. Delicious!

Chocolate Chip Cookies

Ingredients:
- 1 ½ cups all-purpose flour
- 1 tsp. baking soda
- ½ tsp. salt
- ½ cup unsalted butter, softened
- ½ cup packed brown sugar
- 6 Tbsp. granulated sugar
- 1 large egg
- 1 tsp. vanilla extract
- 2 cups semi-sweet chocolate chips

Directions:
- In a large mixing bowl, sift flour, baking soda and salt together.
- In a separate bowl, mix together butter and sugars with a stand mixer until smooth; reduce speed and add egg and vanilla. Gradually add the flour mixture.
- Add chocolate chips and stir in with a wooden spoon.
- Using a heaping tablespoon, spoon mixture onto greased air fryer basket or baking sheet appropriate for your air fryer.
- Cook at 360 for approximately 6 minutes. It will take several batches to get through the mixture, which makes around 18-20 cookies.

Chocolate Soufflé

Ingredients:
- 3 oz. semi-sweet chocolate chips
- ¼ cup sweet cream butter
- 2 eggs, separated
- 3 Tbsp. sugar
- ½ tsp. vanilla extract
- 2 Tbsp. all-purpose flour
- Pinch of powdered sugar for dusting
- Optional: ice cream or whipped cream for topping

Directions:
- Preheat your air fryer to 330 degrees.
- Grease two small ramekins (6 oz.) with butter.
- Melt the chocolate chips with the butter in a double boiler.
- In a medium bowl, beat egg yolks together, adding the sugar and vanilla. Continue to whisk. Then, gradually add the chocolate/butter mixture, mixing until well blended.
- Stir in the flour until the mixture is smooth and free of lumps.
- In a separate bowl, whisk together the egg whites until they have attained peak stage.
- Fold half of the eggs into the chocolate mixture until combined.
- Pour the chocolate mixture into the ramekins, leaving room at the top (about ½ inch).
- Transfer ramekins to the air fryer basket and cook for 14 minutes.
- Serve warm.

Dust tops with powdered sugar and serve with whipped cream or vanilla ice cream. They also look beautiful if you add a sprinkle of cinnamon on the whipped cream or ice cream.

Triple Berry Dessert Egg Rolls

Ingredients:
- ½ cup sugar
- 2 ½ Tbsp. cornstarch
- Dash of salt
- 2 cups blueberries
- 1 cup raspberries
- 1 cup blackberries
- 1 Tbsp. butter
- 1 Tbsp. lemon juice
- Egg roll wrappers
- 1 egg, beaten
- Confectionary sugar

Directions:
- In a medium saucepan, combine sugar, cornstarch, salt, 1 Tbsp. water, 1 cup blueberries, 1 cup raspberries, and ½ cup blackberries. Bring to a boil, stirring for two minutes until thickened.
- Remove from heat and add butter, lemon juice and remaining berries, stirring until butter is melted.
- Let cool.
- Once mixture is cooled, spoon approximately 2 Tbsp. of the berry mixture into the center of the egg roll wrapper (wrapper should be in a diamond shape for proper folding). Fold and seal with beaten egg.
- Cook in air fryer at 390 degrees for 8 minutes, turning halfway through. For added flavor and crispness, brush tops with melted butter at the halfway point.
- Plate and top with a sprinkle of confectionary sugar.

Best served with vanilla ice cream.

Cherry Hand Pies

Ingredients:
- 2 frozen or refrigerated pie crusts
- 2 large cans cherry pie filling
- ¼ cup butter, melted

Instructions:
- Cut pie crust into circles with a pastry ring or knife.
- Spoon cherry pie filling in one side of the circle.
- Fold over, pinching dough to seal along the edges.
- Mist air fryer basket with oil.
- Place hand pie in air fryer basket and brush with melted butter
- Air fry at 360 for 15 minutes, turning once.

Serve with vanilla ice cream.

S'mores

Ingredients
- 4 honey graham crackers
- 2 Hershey's milk chocolate bars
- 1 bag jumbo marshmallows

Directions:
- Preheat air fryer to 400 degrees
- Spear jumbo marshmallows on skewers compatible with your air fryer.
- Place in basket.
- Cook at 400 until marshmallows soften and begin to melt.
- Sandwich the marshmallow and chocolate square between two graham crackers for a delicious treat when there's no campfire!

Ultimate Chocolate Cake

Ingredients:
- 1 box yellow butter cake mix
- 4 large eggs
- 1 large box instant chocolate pudding
- 2/3 cup oil
- 2/3 cup sugar
- 1/3 cup water
- 8 oz. sour cream
- 6 oz. semi-sweet chocolate chips
- Optional: 1 cup chopped nuts

Directions:
- Mix cake mix, pudding, oil, sugar, and water in a stand mixer.
- Add 1 egg at a time, beating well after each.
- Fold in sour cream, chocolate chips, and nuts.
- Distribute mixture in 2-3 greased and floured, air-fryer approved cake pans or Bundt pan.
- "Bake" each layer at 360 for 25-30 minutes.
- Be sure to allow for cooling before you add icing or, if you prefer, ganache.

Note: This cake can be served in 2-3 layers, or you can freeze additional layers and serve in a single layer for fewer servings.

This cake is beautiful topped with chocolate ganache and garnished with fresh berries.

Sour Cream Banana Cake with Caramel Frosting

Ingredients:
- ¼ cup butter
- 1 1/3 cups sugar
- 2 eggs
- 1 tsp. vanilla
- 2 cups sifted all-purpose flour
- 1 tsp. baking powder
- 1 tsp. baking soda
- ¾ tsp. salt
- 1 cup sour cream
- 1 cup mashed ripe bananas (about 2 bananas)
- ½ cup chopped walnuts

Directions:
- In a mixing bowl, cream butter, gradually adding sugar; beat until light and fluffy.
- Add eggs, 1 at a time, and beat until well-mixed.
- Add vanilla.
- In a separate bowl, sift together flour, baking powder, baking soda, and salt;
- Add to creamed mixture, alternating between flour and sour cream, beginning and ending with the dry ingredients.
- Add bananas and nuts, mixing until just blended.
- Distribute into greased, floured, air-fryer compatible Bundt pan.
- Bake at 360 for 25-30 minutes.
- Let cool and top with caramel frosting.

Caramel Frosting

Ingredients:
- ½ cup butter
- ½ cup firmly packed brown sugar
- ¼ cup evaporated milk
- 2 ¼ cup powdered sugar
- 1 tsp. vanilla

Directions:
- In a 1-quart saucepan, heat together butter and brown sugar over low heat, stirring constantly until sugar melts.
- Blend in evaporated milk; let cool.
- Gradually beat in sugar until the mixture reaches "spreading" consistency; stir in vanilla.

Main Dishes

Fish and Chips

Ingredients:
- 3-4 pieces of cod or other white fish
- 1 cup flour
- 2 eggs
- 3/4 cup panko bread crumbs
- 1/4 tsp. Cajun seasoning
- Salt and pepper to taste (most Cajun seasonings already contain salt)
- Make fries, according to our recipe, located in the "sides" section, or use 1/2 bag of frozen.

Directions:
- Sprinkle salt and pepper over fish, as desired.
- Place flour in bowl; set aside.
- Beat eggs in a bowl; set aside.
- In a small bowl, combine panko with Cajun seasoning; set aside.
- Spray basket of air fryer with oil mister or non-stick spray.
- Coat fish in flour, then egg, and finally, the panko mixture. Place in air fryer. Repeat the process until all the fish is coated in the egg wash mixture.
- If there's room in your air fryer, place frozen fries or homemade fries with the fish.
- Cook at 400 degrees for 10 minutes, flipping the fish at five minutes.

Serve with tartar sauce and a side of slaw.

Salmon with Lemon and Rosemary

Ingredients:
- 2-3 fresh or thawed-from-frozen salmon filets
- 1 Tbsp. fresh-squeezed lemon
- 3 Tbsp. of extra virgin olive oil
- 1 Tbsp. of fresh or dried rosemary
- 1/4 tsp. sea salt
- 1/8 tsp. black pepper

Directions:
- In a small bowl, combine all ingredients.
- Brush the mixture onto the salmon.
- Spray air fryer basket with non-stick cooking spray.
- Set the air fryer to the "fish" setting or cook at 400 degrees for 10 minutes, flipping halfway. You may adjust cooking times, according to personal preference--less if you prefer salmon less done or more if you prefer it well done.

Turkey Breast

Ingredients:
- 1 bone-in turkey breast (6 pounds or less, depending on your air fryer capacity)
- 1 Tbsp. olive oil
- ½ tsp. Herbs de Provence
- ¼ tsp. salt

Directions:
- Mix together Herbs de Provence and salt.
- Rub the turkey breast with olive oil. Rub with herb mixture.
- Cook breast-side-down in the air fryer for 40-45 minutes at 360 degrees, turning halfway.

Save the drippings in the bottom of your air fryer for gravy.

Asian Ahi Tuna Steaks

Ingredients:
- 2 ahi tuna steaks
- 1 tsp. grated garlic
- 1 Tbsp. lemon juice
- ¼ cup soy sauce
- 1 Tbsp. sesame oil
- 1 Tbsp. sesame seeds
- 1 scallion, chopped

Directions:
- Preheat air fryer to 360 degrees (about 3-5 minutes).
- Mix together all ingredients, except the tuna steaks and lemon.
- Wash and pat dry tuna steaks, rubbing them with lemon juice, salt, and pepper.
- Cover all sides in the marinade and refrigerate for 2 hours before cooking.
- Cook tuna in air fryer at 360 for 6 minutes, turning once.

Buttermilk Fried Chicken

Ingredients:
- 1-2 pounds bone-in drumsticks or chicken pieces
- 1 quart buttermilk
- Mixture of paprika, and Cajun seasoning (to taste).
- 1 tsp. hot sauce
- Optional: ¼ tsp cayenne pepper (You may find this marinade to be spicy enough.)
- 1 tsp. salt
- ¼ tsp. garlic powder
- ½ tsp. pepper
- 2-3 eggs
- 3-4 cups flour
- 3 Tbsp. buttermilk
- Peanut oil (or vegetable oil, in the event of allergies)

Directions:
- In a large bowl, mix together buttermilk and paprika, Cajun seasoning, hot sauce, and cayenne pepper. Place chicken in the mixture, making sure to cover all the pieces. Cover. Refrigerate overnight to marinate. (If you don't have a large enough bowl, you can also use leak-proof zipper bags.)
- Whisk together egg and buttermilk in a medium sized mixing bowl; set aside.
- In a separate bowl mix together flour, garlic powder, salt, and pepper.
- Dredge the chicken pieces in the egg wash, then thoroughly coat in flour mixture.
- Refrigerate for 30 minutes to help the coating stick to the chicken.
- Spritz the basket of your air fryer with peanut oil. Place the chicken pieces inside (you will need to make a couple of batches if cooking more than a pound). Mist the tops of the chicken pieces with additional peanut oil to lock in the moisture.
- Cook at 400 degrees for 20-23 minutes, turning once.

Note: If you are cooking a variety of chicken pieces, check the wings and drumsticks at about 15 minutes to prevent overcooking.

Calabash Shrimp

Ingredients
- 1 pound medium raw shrimp, cleaned and deveined, tails removed
- ½ cup milk
- 1 egg, beaten
- 1 cup all-purpose flour
- ½ tsp. salt

Directions:
- Mix flour and salt together on a deep plate or shallow baking dish.
- In a separate bowl, mix together milk and egg.
- Dredge shrimp in the egg wash and then coat thoroughly with flour mixture.
- Mist air fryer with oil of your choice. Add shrimp and then mist with additional oil.
- Cook at 330 degrees for 15-17 minutes, shaking at least once.
- Dust with salt.
- Plate and enjoy!

Note: You can use the same batter recipe for calamari.

Italian-Style Meatballs

Ingredients:
- 1 pound ground beef or pork
- 1 egg
- ½ cup Italian bread crumbs
- Salt and pepper, to taste
- 1 tsp. garlic powder
- 1 Tbsp. grated parmesan or Romano cheese

Directions:
- In a large mixing bowl, combine ground beef, egg, bread crumbs, salt, pepper, garlic powder, and cheese.
- Shape into balls and place in air fryer basket in a single layer, spritzing with olive oil.
- Cook in the air fryer at 375 degrees for 15 minutes, turning once.

Great for meatball subs, spaghetti, Italian wedding soup and party appetizers!

Cajun Chicken Strips

Ingredients:
- 1 pound chicken breast tenderloins
- 2 eggs, beaten
- 1 cup all-purpose flour
- 1 tsp. of Cajun seasoning (add more for a spicier flavor or cut for less heat)
- 1/2 tsp. salt (or to taste)
- 1/4 tsp. pepper (or to taste)
- Vegetable cooking spray

Directions:
- In a small bowl, beat two eggs and set aside.
- On a large plate or medium bowl, mix flour, salt, pepper, and Cajun seasoning together.
- Spray the air fryer basket with cooking spray.
- Dip each chicken tenderloin in the egg wash and immediately coat with flour mixture.
- Place coated chicken in a single layer in the air fryer basket. Spray the top of the chicken with cooking spray.
- Cook at 400 degrees for 20 minutes, turning once.

Serve with your favorite dipping sauce.

Chicken Chimichangas

Ingredients:
- 1 pound cooked, shredded chicken
- 1 onion, diced
- 1 small can diced green chilies
- 2 Tbsp. all-purpose flour
- 4-6 oz. of green chili sauce (or 4-6 oz. of red enchilada sauce if you prefer)
- Garlic powder to taste
- Ground cumin to taste
- Chili powder to taste
- Paprika to taste
- 2-4 large tortillas
- Avocado oil

Directions:
- In a large skillet, sauté onion and green chilis in a splash of avocado oil. Add the shredded chicken, garlic powder, cumin, chili powder, and paprika.
- Add flour and sauce, stirring until well-combined.
- Spoon the filling into a warmed tortilla and roll like a burrito.
- Spritz the air fryer basket with avocado oil and place chimichangas in basket.
- Mist the top of the chimichangas with more avocado oil.
- Cook at 400 degrees for 8-10 minutes, flipping once.

Serve with melted queso, lettuce, tomato and guacamole.

Classic Cheeseburgers

Ingredients:
- 1-2 pounds ground chuck or sirloin
- 1-2 Tbsp. of your favorite steak sauce (like A-1)
- Sprinkle of your favorite steak seasoning
- Several slices of your favorite cheese
- Buns
- Toppings (lettuce, tomato, onion, pickles, etc.)

Directions:
- In a large bowl, mix together ground beef with your favorite sauce. Knead together until well-blended.
- Shape into patties of the desired size. Sprinkle patties with your favorite steak seasoning blend.
- Spritz air fryer basket with vegetable oil. Place patties in basket.
- Cook at 390 degrees for 12 minutes, flipping halfway.
- Add cheese and cook for an additional minute or so, until cheese is melted.
- Place on bun and add toppings for a juicy, delicious burger. Enjoy!

To add variety, you can experiment with different cheeses and buns. For example, you can add bacon and use pepper jack cheese, or add mushrooms and swiss. Pretzel buns also provide a delicious alternative to a regular enriched bun.

Crispy Chicken Parmesan

Ingredients:
- 2-4 thin-sliced, boneless, skinless chicken breasts
- 2 cups Italian bread crumbs
- ½ cup grated parmesan cheese
- 2 eggs, beaten
- 1 jar of your favorite spaghetti or marinara sauce
- ½ box dried vermicelli noodles
- Extra parmesan cheese for topping

Directions:
- Rinse and pat dry chicken breasts.
- In a medium bowl or deep plate, mix together Italian bread crumbs and parmesan cheese
- Dredge chicken breasts in the egg wash and then coat in bread crumbs/parmesan mixture.
- Spritz your air fryer with your favorite oil.
- Place chicken in air fryer. Mist tops with oil.
- Cook at 390 for 15-18 minutes, turning once.
- Plate on top of vermicelli, cooked according to package instructions, and top with heated spaghetti sauce. Finish plating with a sprinkle of parmesan cheese.

Coconut Shrimp

Ingredients:
- 1 pound raw shrimp, deveined with tails removed
- 2 cups unsweetened coconut flakes
- 2 cups panko crumbs
- 1 can coconut milk

Directions:
- In a large bowl, mix together coconut and panko crumbs.
- In a separate bowl, pour coconut milk and stir until cream and milk are well-mixed.
- Dredge shrimp in coconut milk and coat in panko/coconut mixture.
- Spray your air fryer basket with melted coconut oil. Place shrimp in a single layer in the air fryer basket. Spritz tops with oil.
- Cook at 330 degrees for 15 minutes, shaking once.

Serve with your favorite dipping sauce.

Cumin-Infused Chicken Thighs

Ingredients
- 8 medium boneless skinless chicken thighs
- Olive oil
- ¼ cup sea salt
- ¼ cup ground cumin
- 1 Tbsp. ground pepper
- 1 Tbsp. rosemary

Directions
- Prepare the rub by mixing the sea salt, cumin, pepper and rosemary together.
- Coat the chicken in a thin layer of olive oil.
- Put the rub in a plastic bag and, one by one, put a chicken thigh in, shaking to coat it thoroughly, and place in the air fryer.
- Once all chicken has been coated, cook in the air fryer for 20 minutes at 390 degrees.

Note: You will need to cook the 8 pieces of chicken in batches. To reduce amount, cut recipe in half.

Bacon-Wrapped Turkey Filets

Ingredients:
- Bacon-wrapped filet
- Olive oil
- Your favorite steak seasoning

Directions:
- Brush each side of filets with olive oil.
- Sprinkle steak seasoning onto each side of filets.
- Place into air fryer and cook for 4 1/2 minutes at 390 degrees.
- Flip filets.
- Cook for another 4 1/2 minutes at 390 degrees.

Pork Chops with Rosemary-Apricot Glaze

Ingredients:
- 4 boneless pork chops
- 1 tsp. rosemary
- Salt and pepper to taste
- ½ jar of apricot preserves

Directions:
- Rub pork chops with salt and pepper; set aside.
- In a small saucepan, stir the apricot preserves together with the rosemary over medium heat until the mixture begins to bubble and become fragrant.
- Spray the basket of your air fryer with your favorite oil.
- Brush both sides of the pork chops with the rosemary apricot glaze.
- Cook at 380 degrees for 20-25 minutes, flipping porkchops at the halfway point.

Note: You can also use this glaze on pork loin or pork roast.

Pair these pork chops with mashed sweet potatoes and a spring mix salad for a delicious fall meal.

Eggplant Parmesan

Ingredients:
- 1 eggplant, skin removed
- 1 cup Italian bread crumbs
- ½ cup parmesan cheese
- 2 eggs, beaten
- Olive oil
- Salt and pepper to taste

Directions:
- Cut eggplant into coins around ¼ inches in thickness.
- Spray both sides of the eggplant with a mist of olive oil. Then, sprinkle each side with salt and pepper. Set aside.
- Mix together bread crumbs and cheese on a large plate or shallow pan.
- Dredge eggplant in egg wash and then coat in bread crumb mixture.
- Spritz air fryer basket with oil and add eggplant. Spritz tops with oil spray.
- Cook at 390 degrees for 30 minutes, flipping at 15 minutes.

Serve with a side of marinara for dipping or over a bed of pasta with spaghetti sauce and parmesan cheese.

Fried Catfish

Ingredients:
- 4-6 catfish filets, rinsed and patted dry
- ½ lemon
- 1 cup of your favorite brand of fish fry (We use Cajun-style fish fry for added spice.)
- Spritz of your favorite oil

Directions:
- Squeeze lemon over catfish filets.
- Coat all sides of filets thoroughly with the fish fry.
- Spritz your air fryer basket with a mist of your favorite oil.
- Place 2-3 filets in your air fryer, depending upon its capacity, and spritz the tops with oil.
- Cook at 390 degrees for 15 minutes, flipping at the 10-minute mark.

Pair this fish with our air fryer hushpuppies, corn on the cob, and golden fries.

Honey Ginger Salmon

Ingredients:
- 2-4 salmon steaks
- ½ fresh lemon
- ¼ cup soy sauce
- ¼ cup honey
- 1 tsp. ground ginger or a ½ inch piece of fresh ginger, peeled and grated
- 1 tsp. minced garlic or 1 clove garlic, minced
- Optional: scallions for garnish

Directions:
- Squeeze lemon juice over the salmon steaks and refrigerate for 30 minutes.
- In a saucepan, mix together soy sauce, honey, ginger, and garlic over medium heat. Stir until bubbly and well-combined.
- Spritz your air fryer basket with sesame oil.
- Remove salmon steaks from the refrigerator and pat dry.
- Glaze with honey ginger sauce and place in air fryer basket (mine holds 2 salmon steaks).
- Spritz top of steaks with a mist of sesame oil.
- Cook at 400 degrees for approximately 10 minutes, turning once. (You may also use your air fryer's fish setting.)
- Remove and plate, garnishing with scallions for added color and flavor. Enjoy!

Serve with steamed rice and asparagus.

Sweet Whiskey-Glazed Country Ribs

Ingredients:
- 2-3 pounds country pork ribs
- 2-3 Tbsp. of your favorite rib rub
- 1 Tbsp. oil
- 1 small onion, diced
- 1 cup of your favorite whiskey
- 1 tsp. dried mustard
- 3 Tbsp. brown sugar
- 1 tsp. Worcestershire sauce
- 1 tsp. lemon juice
- 1 cup ketchup

Directions:
- The day before cooking, rub spare ribs in your favorite rib rub and refrigerate overnight.
- Spritz air fryer basket with your favorite oil. Add ribs and spritz the top of the rubbed ribs with oil.
- Sauté onion in oil until transparent. Set aside.
- Mix together remaining ingredients and add to the sautéed onions. Bring to a boil. Reduce heat and simmer for 15-20 minutes.
- Cook ribs at 350 degrees for 10 minutes, turning halfway through.
- Glaze with Sweet Whiskey Sauce and cook for an additional 5 minutes. Use remaining sauce for dipping.

Kickin' Kebabs

Ingredients:
- 12 oz of sirloin, 2 lbs. of chicken, or 1 pound of shrimp (or all three if you desire)
- 3 bell peppers
- 2 sweet onions
- 1 carton of whole mushrooms
- Your favorite steak, poultry or shrimp seasoning (Creole works well for all three.)

Directions:
- Cut meat into thick chunks and season.
- Cut vegetables into thick chunks or "petals". Leave mushrooms whole.
- Using air fryer-safe skewers, spear meat, followed by one of each vegetable, and repeat until skewer is loaded.
- Cook at 350 for 15-20 minutes, turning halfway.

For sweeter kebabs, add pineapple chunks and glaze the completed skewers with honey.

Lobster Tails for Two

Ingredients:
- 2-4 fresh lobster tails
- 2-4 Tbsp. melted butter
- 1 tsp. garlic
- Salt and pepper to taste
- Optional: parsley for garnish.

Directions:
- Using strong kitchen shears, cut the lobster tail down the middle and peel back. Be careful not to cut your hands. The shells are very sharp!
- In a small saucepan, melt the butter over medium heat, careful not to boil.
- Add the garlic and simmer for five minutes.
- Place the lobster tails in the basket of your air fryer.
- Salt and pepper the exposed meat. Then drizzle with half of the butter mixture.
- Cook at 390 degrees for approximately 5 minutes.
- Pause the air fryer and pour remaining butter mixture over lobster tails.
- Return basket to chamber and cook an additional minute or two.
- Plate and sprinkle with parsley. Enjoy!

Orange Chicken

Ingredients
- 2-4 boneless, skinless chicken breasts, cut into chunks
- ¼ cup soy sauce
- 2 tbsp. honey
- ½ cup orange marmalade
- 1 inch piece of ginger, peeled and sliced
- 2 scallions, chopped
- Salt and pepper to taste

Instructions
- Spray air fryer with a mist of sesame oil. Add the chicken chunks, salting and peppering to taste.
- Cook at 350 for 10-15 minutes, shaking halfway.
- Meanwhile, in a medium sauce pan, combine soy sauce, honey, marmalade, ginger and scallions, stirring often and heating until bubbly.
- Remove chicken from air fryer and add to the sauce.
- Serve over rice and garnish with additional scallions.

Ragin' Cajun Shrimp

Ingredients:
- 1-2 pounds medium shrimp, deveined.
- ½ fresh lemon for squeezing
- Salt and pepper to taste
- 1-2 Tbsp. avocado or olive oil
- 2 tsp. of your favorite Creole seasoning (increase or reduce based on your heat preference)

Directions:
- Rinse the shrimp and pat dry with a paper towel.
- In a large mixing bowl, squeeze lemon juice over shrimp and toss until all shrimp are coated.
- Then toss shrimp in avocado oil until well-coated.
- Mix in salt and pepper to taste, adding the Creole seasoning. Toss until well-coated.
- Place the shrimp in a single layer in your air fryer basket and cook at 350 for 10-15 minutes, turning once.

Roasted Whole Chicken

Ingredients:
- 1 whole chicken (between 5-6 pounds, depending upon your air fryer's capacity)
- A few mists of olive oil from your favorite oil mister
- Salt and pepper to taste
- 1 Tbsp. fresh or dried rosemary leaves
- 1 tsp. thyme
- ½ tsp. sage

Directions:
- Rinse chicken, removing all giblets; pat dry, inside and out, with paper towels.
- Spritz chicken with olive oil and rub with salt and pepper.
- Sprinkle evenly with rosemary, thyme, and sage.
- Place in your air fryer basket and cook at 360 degrees for 1 hour, flipping once; let rest for several minutes before serving.

To add variety, replace the herbs with your favorite chicken seasoning, like lemon pepper, creole or Italian herb.

Sea Scallops

Ingredients:
- 1 pound sea scallops
- A few spritzes of olive oil
- Salt and pepper to taste or a sprinkle of your favorite seasoning

Directions:
- Brush olive oil onto top of scallops.
- Place into air fryer and cook for 2 minutes at 390 degrees.
- Flip scallops to brown on other side.
- Cook for another 2 minutes at 390 degrees.

Stuffed Bell Peppers

Ingredients:
- Four green bell peppers
- 1 pound of ground beef or turkey
- 1 clove garlic, minced
- ½ onion, diced
- ½ cup tomato paste
- 1 tsp. Worcestershire sauce
- Salt and pepper to taste
- ½ cup grated cheddar cheese
- 2 Tbsp. olive oil

Directions:
- Hollow out four green peppers for stuffing; set aside.
- In 2 tsp. olive oil, sauté the garlic and onion over med heat until translucent and fragrant.
- In a large mixing bowl, combine the ground beef or turkey with the cheese, tomato paste, Worcestershire sauce, salt, pepper and onion/garlic mixture.
- Distribute evenly into hollowed out bell peppers.
- Transfer to the air fryer. Cook at 390 for 15-20 minutes, or until cooked through.
- If desired, top with more tomato paste and additional cheese. Return to air fryer for 2-3 minutes to melt the cheese.

Sweet n' Sticky Barbecue Drumsticks

Ingredients:
- 1 family-sized package of chicken drumsticks
- 1 Tbsp. oil
- 1 onion, diced
- 1 tsp. dried mustard
- 3 Tbsp. brown sugar
- 1 tsp. Worcestershire sauce
- 1 tsp. lemon juice
- 1 cup ketchup

Directions:
- In a large saucepan, heat oil and cook diced onion over medium heat until translucent.
- Add all ingredients (except chicken), stirring together over medium heat until sugar is melted.
- Simmer for 15 minutes.
- Place drumsticks in air fryer and cook at 400 degrees for 10 minutes, turning once.
- Toss drumsticks in sauce and air fry for an additional 5 minutes.

Meatloaf

Ingredients:
- 2 pounds ground beef
- ½ cup onion, diced
- ¼ cup green pepper, diced
- 2 large eggs
- ½ cup ketchup
- 1 tsp. mustard
- ½ cup brown sugar
- ¼ tsp. pepper
- 1 tsp. salt
- ½ cup oatmeal
- 4 oz bag of shredded cheddar cheese
- 2/3 cup milk

Directions:
- In a large mixing bowl, combine ground beef, onion, eggs, pepper, salt, oatmeal, cheddar cheese and milk until well mixed.
- In a small saucepan, heat ketchup, mustard and brown sugar, stirring over medium heat until mixture thickens to resemble a glaze.
- Transfer meatloaf mixture into a greased loaf pan compatible with your air fryer.
- Cook at 375 degrees for 30-40 minutes.
- Pour glaze over top of the meatloaf and cook an additional five minutes.
- Let cool.

Sides

Multi-Colored Roasted Potatoes

Ingredients:
- 1 ½ pound bag of multi-colored mini potatoes
- 2 Tbsp. olive oil
- 2 cloves minced garlic
- Salt & pepper to taste
- 1 Tbsp. dried parsley

Directions
- In a large bowl, mix potatoes, olive oil, minced garlic and dried parsley together.
- Add salt and pepper to your taste.
- Cook in air fryer for 15 minutes at 400 degrees.
- At least half way through cooking process, flip potatoes.

Loaded "Baked" Potatoes

Ingredients:
- 2-4 average sized baking potatoes
- Vegetable oil
- Salt and pepper to taste
- 4 Tbsp. butter
- ¼ cup sour cream
- 4 Tbsp. bacon bits
- ½ cup shredded cheddar cheese
- Optional: chives for garnish

Directions:
- Wash potatoes thoroughly and use a knife to cut slits in each side.
- Rub potatoes with oil, salt, and pepper.
- Transfer potatoes to the air fryer.
- Cook at 400 degrees for 30 minutes.
- Slice open each potato and add butter, cheese, and bacon bits.
- Return to air fryer and cook until cheese is melted.
- Top with sour cream and chives.

Bacon-Wrapped Asparagus

Ingredients:
- 1 bunch of fresh asparagus
- 1 Tbsp. olive oil
- 1 pound of your favorite bacon
- Salt and pepper to taste

Directions:
- In a large mixing bowl or shallow pan, toss asparagus with olive oil, salt and pepper together until thoroughly coated.
- Wrap each asparagus stalk in one strip of bacon.
- Spritz your air fryer basket with oil
- Place asparagus inside and cook at 360 degrees for 8-10 minutes or until desired crispness is achieved.

"Baked" Sweet Potatoes with Cinnamon and Brown Sugar

Ingredients:
- 4 average sized sweet potatoes (yams)
- Coconut oil
- 1 Tbsp. cinnamon
- 1 Tbsp. brown sugar
- 4 Tbsp. butter

Directions:
- Using a knife, cut slits into each side of the potatoes.
- Rub sweet potatoes with coconut oil
- Place in air fryer basket and cook at 400 degrees for 25-30 minutes.
- Cut open each potato and fill with 1 Tbsp. of butter.
- Once butter has melted, sprinkle each potato with brown sugar and cinnamon.

Note: If you are a fan of marshmallows, you can add a handful of mini-marshmallows, return to the air fryer and cook for an additional minute or two, until marshmallows have melted.

Zesty Curly Fries

Ingredients:
- 2-3 potatoes
- Olive oil
- Salt and Pepper, to taste
- 1 tsp. Cajun seasoning

Directions:
- Wash and peel the potatoes.
- Using a vegetable spiralizer, cut the potatoes into curls.
- Toss in olive oil, salt, pepper and Cajun seasoning.
- Transfer to basket of your air fryer.
- Cook at 400 degrees for 20-25 minutes, shaking halfway through.

Beer-Battered Onion Rings

Ingredients:
- 2 large Vidalia onions
- 1 cup all-purpose flour
- 1 cup of your favorite beer
- ½ tsp. garlic powder
- ½ tsp. onion powder
- ½ tsp. black pepper
- 1 tsp. salt
- Spritz of peanut oil

Directions:
- Slice onions into rings.
- Mix together flour and beer.
- Add remaining ingredients, mixing until well blended.
- Dredge onion rings in the batter and place in the oiled air fryer basket.
- Cook at 390 degrees for 6-8 minutes, shaking halfway.

Brussels Sprouts with Honey-Balsamic Marinade

Ingredients:
- 1 pound of Brussels sprouts
- 1 Tbsp. of balsamic vinegar
- 1 Tbsp. of honey
- Salt and pepper to taste
- 1 Tbsp. olive oil

Directions:
- Thoroughly wash Brussels sprouts and cut them into halves or quarters.
- Mix olive oil with salt and pepper to taste.
- Toss sprouts with olive oil mixture.
- Transfer to air fryer and cook at 400 degrees for 10 minutes, shaking once.
- Mix together vinegar and honey, then toss brussels sprouts with mixture.

Old-Fashioned French Fries

Ingredients
- 2 large russet potatoes
- 1 Tbsp. olive oil
- ½ tsp. sea salt

Directions
- Cut the potatoes into long strips of your desired thickness (a mandoline slicer works best).
- Toss the fries in oil and place them in the air fryer.
- Cook at 400 degrees for 25-30 minutes until or until they are nearly done. Add the salt and cook for another 5 minutes. For extra crispy fries, cook for a total of 40 minutes.

Green Beans with Garlic & Sage

Ingredients:
- 1 pound fresh green beans
- 1 ½ Tbsp. minced garlic
- 1 to 2 tsp. chopped sage leaves
- 1 to 2 tsp. seasoned salt
- 2 Tbsp. olive oil

Directions:
- Mix green beans with garlic, sage, olive oil and seasoned salt.
- Air fry for 8 minutes at 400 degrees.
- Pull out and shake basket once or twice during cooking.

Panko Parmesan Broccoli

Ingredients:
- 3 heads of broccoli
- 2 Tbsp. avocado oil
- ¼ tsp. salt
- 1 tsp. garlic powder
- 1 tsp. Italian seasoning
- ¼ cup parmesan cheese
- ¼ cup panko bread crumbs

Directions:
- Cut the broccoli into medium size heads, removing the stalks.
- Put broccoli into bowl and combine avocado oil.
- Mix panko bread crumbs, parmesan cheese, salt, garlic powder and Italian seasoning with broccoli.
- Mix well.
- Put mixture into air fryer for 12 minutes at 190 Degrees. Stir half way through.

Roasted Corn on the Cob

Ingredients:
- 2 large ears of corn, cut in half
- A few sprays of vegetable oil
- Salt and pepper to taste

Directions:
- Wash corn and pat dry.
- Spritz with oil, thoroughly coating the corn.
- Rub with salt and pepper.
- Place in air fryer basket and cook at 400 degrees for 10 minutes, flipping at the 5-minute mark.

Sweet Potato Fries

Ingredients
- 3 medium sweet potatoes
- 2 Tbsp. olive oil
- 1 tsp. salt

Directions
- Cut the sweet potatoes into long "fry-like" strips.
- Mix the salt and pepper in with the olive oil.
- Add the oil mixture to the air fryer as well and turn it on.
- Cook the fries in the air fryer for about 22 minutes at 400 degrees.
- Check them for desired crispiness - it can take up to 35 minutes for them to become crispy because they are more dense than normal French fries.
- Be sure to flip them halfway through the cooking process to make sure you get an even cook.

For a sweeter flavor, replace olive oil with coconut oil and salt with cinnamon.

Squash & Zucchini with Onions

Ingredients:
- 2 medium zucchinis
- 2 medium yellow squash
- 1 yellow onion
- 4 Tbsp. olive oil
- ¼ tsp. salt
- ¼ tsp. garlic powder
- ¼ tsp. ground black pepper

Directions:
- Cut the zucchini and yellow squash in ¼-inch slices.
- Combine zucchini, yellow squash and olive oil.
- Mix in the salt, garlic powder, and black pepper.
- Put in air fryer for 15 minutes at 400 degrees.
- While the zucchini and yellow squash cook, dice the yellow onion.
- When zucchini and yellow squash done, add the diced yellow onion.
- Cook all for 10 minutes at 400 degrees.

Holiday Bonus Menus

Honey Glazed Spiral Ham

Ingredients:
- 1 pre-cooked spiral glazed honey ham
- Provided glaze

Directions:
- If your ham doesn't fit, cut the ham off the bone.
- Cook ham for 15 minutes at 300 degrees.
- While the ham is doing its initial cook, prepare the glaze per directions.
- When ham finishes, take out and rotate the top half of your ham slices to the bottom of the pan and the bottom half to the top.
- While rotating the ham, brush on glaze as you place ham back in the air fryer.
- Cook ham for 15 more minutes at 300 degrees.
- Take out, make sure hot throughout all layers in the basket then enjoy!

Holiday Tips:
- Garnish ham with pineapple and cherries.
- Serve on a beautiful white platter or holiday appropriate platter.
- Best served with sweeter wines, like Riesling or Moscato.
- Perfect for Thanksgiving, Christmas, Easter and Mother's Day.

Turkey Breast

Ingredients:
- 1 bone-in turkey breast (6 lbs. or less, depending on your air fryer capacity)
- 1 Tbsp. olive oil
- ½ tsp. Herbs de Provence
- ¼ tsp. salt

Directions:
- Mix together Herbs de Provence and salt.
- Rub the turkey breast with olive oil then rub with herb mixture.
- Cook breast-side down in the air fryer for 40-45 minutes at 360 degrees, turning halfway.

You can save the drippings in the bottom of your air fryer for gravy.

Holiday Tips:
- If serving for Thanksgiving, pair this delicious turkey breast with Orange-Cranberry Stuffing and garnish the platter with fresh, fragrant herbs, like rosemary, thyme and sage. For color, add whole cranberries to the platter.
- If serving for Christmas, garnish with sugar-coated cranberries and holly leaves.
- Best wines with turkey dinner: if you prefer reds, try a nice Bordeaux or Pinot Noir, and if you prefer whites, try a Chardonnay or Riesling.
- Also perfect for Mother's Day and Easter.

Apple-Bourbon Cornish Hens

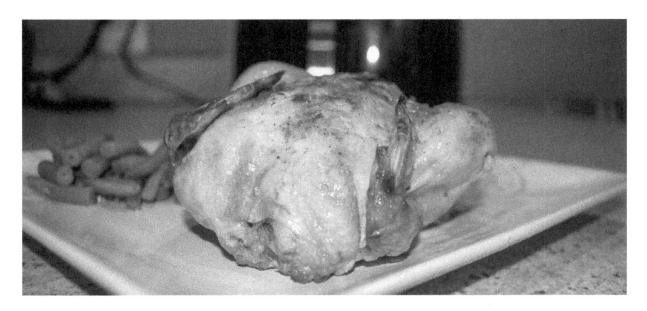

Ingredients:
- 1-2 Cornish game hens
- ½ cup bourbon
- 1 cup apple cider
- 2 Tbsp. butter
- ¼ tsp. cinnamon
- ¼ tsp. nutmeg
- 1/8 tsp. allspice
- Pinch of ground cloves
- 1 Tbsp. brown sugar

Directions:
- In a medium saucepan, stir together spices, sugar, cider and bourbon.
- Cook, stirring frequently until liquid reduces. Add butter and melt, stirring until mixture takes on a "glaze" texture. Taste and adjust seasonings to your liking.
- Spritz the basket of your air fryer with oil and preheat to 400 degrees.
- Rub the game hen with olive oil, salt and pepper. Place in the air fryer.
- Cook at 400 degrees for 30 minutes, turning once. Pause.
- Baste the game hen with the apple bourbon glaze. Return to air fryer, glazed side up. Cook for an additional 15 minutes.

Holiday Tips:
- Pairs nicely with a holiday bourbon-based cocktail or rosé wine.

Lamb Chops with Mint Jelly

Ingredients:
- 8 lamb chops (for larger parties, double recipe; you will have to air fry in batches)
- Several spritzes of olive oil
- 1 Tbsp. dried or fresh rosemary
- Salt and pepper to taste
- Mint jelly

Directions:
- Rub the lamb with oil, rosemary, and salt and pepper.
- Spritz your air fryer basket with olive oil and place lamb chops in batches of 2-4, depending upon your air fryer's capacity.
- Cook at 390 degrees for 5 minutes, turning over at the 2 ½ minute mark.
- Keep warm while you roast the other chops.
- Serve with mint jelly.

Holiday Tips:
- Wine recommendation: Serve with your favorite merlot to compliment the mint sauce.
- Garnish with fresh mint leaves on a beautiful holiday platter.
- These lamb chops are the perfect dish to serve at Christmas or New Year's Eve.

Duck with Orange Sauce

Ingredients:
- 1 duck no more than 5 ½ pounds for a large capacity air fryer
- 1 Tbsp. sesame oil
- Salt and pepper to taste
- Orange sauce glaze (typically comes with the duck)

Directions:
- Preheat your air fryer to 400 degrees.
- Rinse duck and pat dry, removing all giblets.
- Rub with sesame oil, salt and pepper
- Roast duck at 400 degrees for 15 minutes; reduce heat to 360 and cook for an additional 35 minutes.
- Pause air fryer and baste duck with the orange sauce then cook at 360 for an additional 10 minutes.
- Serve with leftover orange sauce.

Holiday Tips:
- Perfect for a Christmas or New Year's Eve feast with family and friends.
- Wine recommendation: Pair with Pinot Noir or Bordeaux.
- Serve on a nice platter and garnish with apples or orange slices.

Pork Tenderloin

Ingredients:
- 1 pork tenderloin
- ½ cup cinnamon apple butter
- Salt and pepper to taste
- 1 Tbsp. of your favorite oil (for rub)
- Apple slices for garnish

Directions:
- Rub pork tenderloin with oil, salt, and pepper.
- With a basting brush, apply a thin layer of apple butter to all sides of the roast.
- Add to air fryer and cook at 360 degrees for 30 minutes, turning once.
- Serve with apple butter.

Holiday Tips:
- This delicious pork tenderloin makes a great alternative to the typical honey glazed ham served at Thanksgiving or Christmas. If you host large parties and offer both ham and turkey, this pork tenderloin makes a great option in place of the turkey.
- For Thanksgiving, Christmas, or New Year's Day, garnish with cooked cinnamon apples.
- Wine recommendation: a nice Chardonnay or light red wine pair nicely with pork.

Mummy Dogs

Ingredients:
- 4-5 of your favorite brand hot dogs
- 1 can crescent rolls

Directions:
- Roll out the crescent rolls and cut into small strips.
- Wrap around hot dogs, leaving a small space for the mummy's eyes.
- Spritz your air fryer basket with vegetable oil.
- Place Mummy Dogs in air fryer.
- Cook at 350 degrees for 10-12 minutes.
- Use candy eyes or two small dots of ketchup, mustard or relish pieces for the eyes.
- Plate and enjoy for a spooky Halloween treat!

Holiday Tips:
- Mummy Dogs are great for parties or at-home Halloween meals.
- Serve with mustard and ketchup for dipping.
- For extra fun, serve on spooky Halloween plates.

Sweet Whiskey-Glazed Country Ribs

Ingredients:
- 2-3 pounds country pork ribs
- 2-3 Tbsp. of your favorite rib rub
- 1 Tbsp. oil
- 1 small onion, diced
- 1 cup of your favorite whiskey
- 1 tsp. dried mustard
- 3 Tbsp. brown sugar
- 1 tsp. Worcestershire sauce
- 1 tsp. lemon juice
- 1 cup ketchup

Directions:
- The day before cooking, rub spare ribs in your favorite rib rub and refrigerate overnight.
- Spritz air fryer basket with your favorite oil. Add ribs and spritz the top of the rubbed ribs with oil.
- Sauté onion in oil until transparent. Set aside.
- Mix together remaining ingredients and add to the sautéed onions. Bring to a boil. Reduce heat and simmer for 15-20 minutes.
- Cook ribs at 350 degrees for 10 minutes, turning halfway through.
- Glaze with Sweet Whiskey Sauce and cook for an additional 5 minutes. Use remaining sauce for dipping.

Holiday Tips:
- Perfect for Memorial Day, Fourth of July and Father's Day.

Classic Cheeseburgers

Ingredients:
- 1-2 pounds ground chuck or sirloin
- 1-2 Tbsp. of your favorite steak sauce
- Sprinkle of your favorite steak seasoning
- Several slices of your favorite cheese
- Buns
- Toppings (lettuce, tomato, onion, pickles, etc.)

Directions:
- In a large bowl, mix together ground beef with your favorite sauce. Knead together until well-blended.
- Shape into patties of the desired size. Sprinkle patties with your favorite steak seasoning blend.
- Spritz air fryer basket with vegetable oil. Place patties in basket.
- Cook at 390 degrees for 12 minutes, flipping halfway.
- Add cheese and cook for an additional minute or so, until cheese is melted.
- Place on bun and add toppings for a juicy, delicious burger. Enjoy!

Holiday Tips:
- For Fourth of July or Memorial Day, and also great for a Father's Day meal.

Hot Dogs

Ingredients:
- 5-8 of your favorite brand of hot dogs (we use nitrate/nitrite free)
- 1 large jar of your favorite sauerkraut
- Relish
- Ketchup
- Mustard
- Hot dog chili
- Diced onions
- Buns

Directions:
- Place hot dogs inside air fryer.
- Cook for 5 minutes at 400 degrees, turning once.
- Place in bun and top with all your favorites!

Holiday Tips:
- Serve on festive patriotic plates for Fourth of July and Memorial Day holidays.
- Serve with baked beans, corn on the cob, and/or chips, as well as a wedge of watermelon.
- Pair with your favorite craft beer.
- Also perfect for a Father's Day celebration.

Healthy Turkey Burgers

Ingredients:
- 1-2 pounds ground turkey
- 1-2 Tbsp. Dijon mustard
- Salt and pepper to taste
- 1 tsp. onion powder
- ½ tsp. garlic powder
- 1 avocado, sliced
- Lettuce, tomato and avocado for topping

Directions:
- In a large mixing bowl, combine ground turkey, mustard, salt, pepper, onion powder, and garlic powder until well mixed.
- Shape into patties.
- Spritz air fryer basket with avocado oil.
- Cook burgers, 2-3 at a time (depending on the capacity of your air fryer), for 10-12 minutes at 390, flipping halfway through the cooking process.
- Plate on a whole wheat bun and top with avocado slices, lettuce and tomato.

Holiday Tips:
- Serve with blueberry and strawberry mixed fruit for a healthier alternative on Memorial Day or the Fourth of July.

Bacon-Wrapped Filets with Sea Scallops

Ingredients:
- 2 bacon-wrapped filets
- 1 pound of sea scallops
- Olive oil
- Your favorite steak seasoning
- Salt, pepper and ½ lemon

Directions for Filets:
- Brush each side of the steak with olive oil
- Sprinkle steak seasoning on each side of the filets
- Cook at 390 degrees for 9 minutes, flipping once.

Directions for Sea Scallops:
- Brush all sides of the scallops with olive oil
- Sprinkle with salt, pepper and lemon juice.
- Cook at 390 degrees for 4 minutes, flipping halfway.

Holiday Tips:
- This meal is an elegant choice for Valentine's Day or a romantic date night.
- Serve with steamed asparagus and fingerling potatoes.
- Dress the table for the occasion with linen tablecloth, your best china or dishes, and drippy candles to impress the special someone in your life.
- Wine Recommendation: Serve with Cabernet Sauvignon, Pinot Noir or Merlot.

Orange Cranberry Stuffing

Ingredients:
- 1 cup dried cranberries
- ½ cup orange-flavored liqueur or orange juice
- 1 pound mild ground pork sausage
- 2 cups coarsely chopped celery
- ¾ cup chopped onion
- ¼ cup butter
- 1 (14 oz.) can of chicken broth
- ½ tsp. salt
- ¼ tsp. pepper
- ½ tsp. dried thyme
- 1 (6 oz) package pork stuffing mix (like Stove Top)
- 1 Tbsp. grated orange rind
- 1 cup chopped pecans

Directions:
- Combine cranberries and liqueur (or juice) in a small saucepan; bring to a boil over medium-high heat. Remove and set aside.
- Brown sausage in a large skillet, stirring until it crumbles; drain, reserving 1 Tbsp. drippings in skillet. Set sausage aside.
- Cook celery and onions in sausage drippings over medium-high heat for 10 minutes; add butter and stir constantly until butter melts.
- Combine cranberry mixture, sausage, stuffing mix and seasoning, orange rind, and pecans in a large mixing bowl, stirring well.
- Transfer stuffing to a small baking dish compatible with your air fryer.
- Cook at 325 degrees for 15 minutes.

Holiday Tips:
- This stuffing is delicious and pairs nicely with Thanksgiving turkey or a crown roast of pork served for Christmas or New Year's Eve.

Sweet Potato Casserole

Ingredients:
- 3 medium-size sweet potatoes
- ¼ cup firmly packed brown sugar
- 1 large egg
- ½ tsp. vanilla extract
- ¼ cup half and half
- ¼ cup butter, melted
- ½ cup firmly packed brown sugar
- 1 Tbsp. all-purpose flour
- 1/8 cup butter
- ½ cup coarsely chopped pecans

Directions:
- Cook sweet potatoes in boiling water until tender; let cool. Once cool, peel and mash.
- Combine sweet potato, ¼ cup brown sugar and next 4 ingredients; beat at medium speed with an electric mixer until smooth.
- Spoon into a greased, air-fryer safe dish.
- Combine ½ cup brown sugar and flour; cut in 1/8 cup butter with a pastry blender until mixture is crumbly.
- Stir in pecans; sprinkle over casserole.
- Cook in air fryer at 350 for 15-18 minutes, or until bubbly.

Holiday Tips:
- It's delicious on any occasion, but most appropriate for Thanksgiving with traditional fall spices.

Okra

Ingredients:
- 1 pound of okra, cut into small coins
- ½ cup buttermilk
- 1 cup corn meal
- Salt and pepper to taste

Directions:
- Combine corn meal, salt and pepper in a mixing bowl.
- Dip okra coins in buttermilk.
- Dredge in cornmeal.
- Place in air fryer basket spritzed with oil.
- Cook at 400 for 12-15 minutes or until okra reaches desired crispness.

Holiday Tips:
- Perfect for Thanksgiving, Kwanzaa.

Corn Pudding

Ingredients:
- 1 box corn muffin mix
- 1 can creamed corn
- 2 cans corn (undrained)
- 1 cup sour cream
- 1 egg
- 1 stick butter, melted
- ¼ cup sugar

Directions:
- Preheat air fryer to 325 degrees.
- Spray an air fryer-safe casserole dish or pan.
- Mix all ingredients together and pour into dish.
- Sprinkle additional sugar on top.
- Cook in air fryer for 50-55 minutes.
- Plate and enjoy!

Holiday Tip:
- Perfect for Thanksgiving and Easter.

Collard Greens

Ingredients:
- 1 bag or bunch of collard greens, stems removed.
- 4 slices bacon or ham, chopped
- ¼ cup onion, diced
- Salt and pepper, to taste
- 1 Tbsp. avocado oil

Directions:
- Wash collard greens thoroughly and pat dry with paper towels
- In a large mixing bowl, toss cut collards, bacon and onion with avocado oil, salt and pepper until well coated with the oil and all ingredients are combined.
- Spray basket of air fryer with a few spritzes of avocado oil.
- Cook at 350 for 15-20 minutes or until greens have reached the desired texture.
- Serve with vinegar.
- Plate and enjoy!

Holiday Tips:
- Perfect for Kwanzaa and New Year's Day.

Honey-Glazed Carrots

Ingredients:
- 1 pound of baby carrots
- 2 Tbsp. butter
- 2 Tbsp. honey
- 1 Tbsp. lemon juice
- Salt and pepper to taste
- Optional: parsley for garnish

Directions:
- In a small saucepan, melt butter over medium heat; add honey and lemon juice, stirring until it reaches a "glaze" consistency.
- In a separate bowl, toss carrots in the glaze until well coated.
- Spritz your air fryer with your favorite oil and add the carrots.
- Air fry at 360 degrees for 12 minutes, shaking once.
- Pour in serving bowl and sprinkle with chopped parsley.

Holiday Tip:
- These delicious glazed carrots are perfect for Thanksgiving, Christmas and Easter.

Baked Beans

Ingredients:
- 2 cups dried navy or white beans, soaked overnight
- 4-5 strips of bacon, chopped
- 1 onion, chopped
- 2 cloves garlic, minced
- ¼ cup molasses
- ¼ cup tomato paste
- ¼ cup brown sugar, packed
- 2 Tbsp. apple cider vinegar
- 1 tsp. mustard powder
- 1 tsp. salt

Directions:
- Mix all ingredients together in a medium mixing bowl.
- Transfer to an air fryer compatible pan.
- Cook at 350 degrees for 5-8 minutes.

Holiday Tip:
- Make these ahead to better meld the flavors together then heat up day of.

Garlic Parmesan Corn on the Cob

Ingredients:
- 8 mini pieces corn on the cob
- ½ stick of butter, melted
- ¼ cup grated parmesan cheese
- 1 Tbsp. parsley, chopped
- Salt and pepper to taste

Directions:
- Mix together melted butter, cheese, parsley, and salt and pepper.
- With a basting brush, thoroughly coat all sides of corn with mixture.
- Place corn in the air fryer.
- Cook at 400 degrees for 10 minutes.
- Baste with leftover butter mixture when done.

Potato Latkes

Ingredients:
- 3 large potatoes, shredded
- 1-2 Tbsp. of your favorite oil
- ¼ cup onion, finely chopped
- 2 eggs
- 1/3 cup bread crumbs
- ¼ cup flour
- Salt and pepper, to taste

Directions:
- Peel potatoes and, using a vegetable grater or mandoline slicer, shred the potatoes into a large mixing bowl.
- Add onion to the potatoes.
- In a separate bowl, beat eggs then add to the potato mixture.
- Stir to combine.
- Add the bread crumbs, flour, salt and pepper, stirring until well combined.
- With oiled hands, pat mixture into individual rounds. Place in an oiled air fryer basket and spritz the tops of the latkes with your favorite oil.
- Cook at 350 degrees for 10 minutes, flipping once.

Holiday Tips:
- Serve with yogurt, sour cream, horseradish or applesauce.
- Perfect for Hanukkah.

Holiday Sugar Cookies

Ingredients:
- 2 ½ cups all-purpose flour
- ½ tsp. baking soda
- 1 tsp. baking powder
- 1 cup salted butter
- 1 ¼ cups granulated sugar
- 3 egg yolks
- 1 tsp. vanilla extract
- Additional sugar for rolling, if desired

Directions:
- Combine flour, baking soda and baking powder in a medium mixing bowl. Set aside.
- Using a hand or stand mixture, beat together butter and sugar.
- Add egg yolks and vanilla extract.
- Add flour mixture, careful to avoid overmixing.
- Scoop dough into balls and roll in sugar; place on air fryer-safe baking pan.
- Bake at 350 for 7-9 minutes.
- Cool on wire racks.
- Decorate.

Holiday Tips:
- For Christmas, use red or green colored sugar for rolling.
- For Christmas, use holiday sprinkles and icing.
- For Halloween, you can add a few drops of orange or green food coloring to the batter for spooky sugar cookies.
- For Halloween, decorate with spooky icing, spider sprinkles, candy corns, or eye balls.

Honey Cake

Ingredients:
- 3 ½ cups flour
- 1 Tbsp. baking powder
- 1 tsp. baking soda
- 1 tsp. cinnamon
- ½ tsp. ginger
- ¼ tsp. nutmeg
- ¼ tsp. cloves
- 1 tsp. baking soda
- 1 ¼ cups brown sugar
- 4 Tbsp. vegetable oil
- 1 ¾ cup honey
- 4 large eggs
- 1 cup coffee
- 1 cup almonds, chopped or sliced (optional)
- 1 cup raisins (optional)

Directions:
- Preheat air fryer to 350.
- In a large mixing bowl, mix eggs, brown sugar, and oil.
- Meanwhile, in a saucepan, combine honey and coffee and bring to a boil. Cool and set aside.
- In a separate bowl, sift together flour, baking powder, baking soda, and cinnamon, ginger, nutmeg, and cloves.
- Beginning and ending with the liquid, stir the honey mixture and flour mixture into the egg mixture.
- If using, stir in raisins and almonds.
- Pour into mini loaf pans.
- Cook at 350 for 25 minutes.
- Cool on wire racks.

Holiday Tips:
- Perfect for Rosh Hashanah
- Drizzle with additional honey.

Cranberry Swirl Cheesecake

Ingredients:
- 1 ¾ cups Bordeaux cookie crumbs
- 2 Tbsp. butter, melted
- 1-pound cream cheese, softened
- 2/3 cup sugar
- ½ tsp. vanilla extract
- 2 tsp. cornstarch
- 2 eggs
- 1 16 oz. can whole berry cranberry sauce
- 1 ¼ tsp. cinnamon
- 1/8 tsp. ground cloves

Directions:
- Use food processor or blender to make Bordeaux cookie crumbs.
- Combine cookie crumbs and melted butter; stir well.
- Press crumb mix onto bottom and 1" up sides of lightly greased 7" springform pan. Bake at 350 degrees for 4 minutes.
- Position knife blade in food processor bowl. Add cranberry sauce and spices; process until smooth. Set aside.
- Beat cream cheese at medium speed of an electric mixer until smooth. Add sugar and cornstarch; beat well. Add eggs, one at a time, beating until just until blended after each addition. Stir in vanilla.
- Pour half of batter into cookie crust; spoon ½ cup cranberry mix over batter. Swirl gently with knife. Top with remaining batter. Spoon ½ cup cranberry mix over cheesecake and swirl gently with knife.
- Bake at 360 degrees for 10 min.
- Reduce heat. Bake at 340 degrees for 10 minutes.
- Reduce heat. Bake at 330 degrees for 15 minutes.
- Remove from air fryer and immediately run a knife around the sides of cheesecake to loosen from pan. Turn off heat and return to air fryer basket to cool for 1 hour.
- Let cool completely in pain on wire rack. Chill, uncovered, until ready to serve.

Holiday Tips:
- This cake is so beautiful, it doesn't need much decoration. However, to dress up for Thanksgiving, garnish with fresh cranberries on top and around the bottom sides.
- For Christmas, garnish with sugared cranberries and holly leaves.

Baked Apples or Pears

Ingredients:
- 2 large apples or 4 pears
- 4 Tbsp. chopped walnuts
- 4 Tbsp. raisins or dried cranberries
- 2 Tbsp. butter, melted
- ½ tsp. cinnamon
- ½ tsp. nutmeg
- ¼ cup water
- ½ tsp. sugar

Directions:
- Cut the apples or pears in half and scoop out core and some of the flesh.
- In a small bowl, combine the walnuts, raisins or cranberries, butter, cinnamon, nutmeg and sugar.
- Place apples/pears inside an air fryer-safe pan and pour in water.
- Spoon walnut mixture inside scooped out apple or pear.
- Cook at 350 degrees for 20 minutes.

Chocolate Soufflé

Ingredients:
- 3 oz. semi-sweet chocolate chips
- ¼ cup sweet cream butter
- 2 eggs, separated
- 3 Tbsp. sugar
- ½ tsp. vanilla extract
- 2 Tbsp. all-purpose flour
- Pinch of powdered sugar for dusting
- Optional: Ice cream or whipped cream for topping

Directions:
- Preheat your air fryer to 330 degrees
- Grease 2 small ramekins (6 oz) with butter.
- Melt the chocolate chips with the butter in a double boiler or in the microwave.
- In a medium bowl, whisk egg yolks together, adding the sugar and vanilla. Continue to whisk. Then, gradually add the chocolate/butter mixture, mixing until well blended.
- Stir in the flour until the mixture is smooth and free of lumps.
- In a separate bowl, whisk together the egg whites until they have attained peak stage.
- Fold half of the eggs into the chocolate mixture until combined.
- Pour the chocolate mixture into the ramekins, leaving room at the top (about ½ inch).
- Transfer ramekins to the air fryer basket and cook for 14 minutes.
- Dust tops with powdered sugar and serve with whipped cream or vanilla ice cream. They also look beautiful if you add a sprinkle of cinnamon on the whipped cream or ice cream.

Holiday Tips:
- For Thanksgiving, plate with a dusting of cinnamon, powdered sugar and cinnamon sticks for garnish.
- For Christmas, add a dollop of whipped cream with sugared cranberries or raspberries with mint leaves or holly.

Red Velvet Cake

Ingredients:
- 1 ½ cups sugar
- 1 cup oil
- 2 eggs
- 1 tsp. vinegar
- 2 oz. red food coloring
- 2 ½ cups all-purpose flour
- 2 Tbsp. cocoa
- 1 tsp. salt
- 1 tsp. baking soda
- 1 cup buttermilk
- 1 tsp. vanilla

Directions:
- Beat together sugar, oil and eggs.
- Stir in vinegar and food coloring.
- In a separate mixing bowl, sift together flour, cocoa, salt, and baking soda.
- Add dry ingredients slowly to first mixture, alternating with the buttermilk.
- Add vanilla.
- Pour batter into 2-3 greased and floured air-fryer compatible cake pans.
- Bake at 325 degrees for 30-35 minutes.
- Cool for 10 minutes on a wire rack.
- Remove cakes from pan and return to wire rack to cool completely.
- Once cool, ice with vanilla or cream cheese frosting.

Holiday Tips:
- Top with fresh blueberries for Memorial Day or Fourth of July.
- For a Christmas dessert, sprinkle top of cake with bits of crushed candy cane or peppermints and decorating sugar. Garnish with peppermint sticks and mint leaves.

Pumpkin Soufflé

Ingredients
- ½ cup sugar
- ½ cup butter
- 3 large eggs, separated
- 1 ½ cups pumpkin puree
- 1 cup milk
- ½ cup cake flour
- 2 tsp. baking powder
- ½ tsp pumpkin pie spice
- Extra cinnamon and confectionary sugar for dusting tops

Directions
- Preheat air fryer to 330 degrees.
- Beat sugar butter, and eggs together until smooth and creamy.
- Add pumpkin puree and mix well.
- Beat milk, flour, and baking powder in pumpkin mixture until smooth.
- Pour into ramekins, leaving room at the top (about ½ inch).
- Cook for 15 minutes.
- Remove from air fryer and dust tops with confectionary sugar.
- Add a dollop of whipped cream with a sprinkle of cinnamon.

Holiday Tips:
- Great personal-sized dessert for guests at your Thanksgiving table.
- Garnish with cinnamon sticks and whipped cream.

Cream Puffs

Ingredients:
- Frozen puff pastry, thawed
- 1 1/3 cups heavy cream
- 1/4 cup powdered sugar
- 1 tsp. vanilla extract
- Optional: whipped cream and berries for topping

Directions:
- Cut thawed puff pastry into circles, using a cookie cutter/dough cutter (9-inch rounds).
- Cook pastry rounds in air fryer at 390 degrees for 8-10 minutes.
- Place on wire racks and allow to cool completely.
- While puff pastry cools, prepare the filling. In a large bowl, whip the heavy whipping cream until it peaks. Whisk in the vanilla and sugar, mixing until peaks are slightly stiff.
- Once pastry cools, either split pastry rounds in half and "sandwich" with cream or, using a piping bag, poke holes in the center of the puffs and fill with cream.
- Top with a sprinkle of powdered sugar, whipped cream and/or berries.

Holiday Tips:
- If serving at Thanksgiving, consider adding pumpkin pie spice to the filling.
- You can also add a zig zag of chocolate icing.
- If serving for Easter, add pink, light blue or green food coloring to the whipped cream.

Patriot Fruit Pizza

Ingredients:
- 1 package/tube of your favorite brand of sugar cookie dough
- 1-2 cups blueberries
- 2-3 cups strawberries, cut in half
- 8 oz. cream cheese, softened
- ¼ cup sugar
- ½ tsp. vanilla

Directions:
- Cut cookie dough in half and roll into two 7-inch circles.
- Press one circle into air fryer pizza attachment.
- Cook cookie dough at 375 degrees for 7-8 minutes.
- Remove; let cool on a wire rack.
- While crust is cooling, mix together cream cheese, vanilla and sugar with a hand or stand mixer.
- Once crust has cooled, spread onto cookie crust.
- Top with strawberries and blueberries, creating a red, white and blue design.
- Repeat with the remaining cookie dough, cheese mixture and fruit.

Holiday Tips:
- Perfect for summer holiday parties and potlucks.

CPSIA information can be obtained
at www.ICGtesting.com
Printed in the USA
LVHW102148100820
662860LV00008B/192